TEACHER'S PET PUBLICATIONS

PUZZLE PACK
for
Harry Potter and the Sorcerer's Stone

based on the book by
J. K. Rowling

Written by
William T. Collins

© 2005 Teacher's Pet Publications
All Rights Reserved

The materials in this packet are copyrighted by Teacher's Pet Publications, Inc.

These pages may be duplicated by the purchaser for use in the purchaser's own classroom.

Copying any of these materials and distributing them for any other purpose is a violation of the copyright laws.

© 2005 Teacher's Pet Publications, Inc.
www.tpet.com

INTRODUCTION
If you already own the LitPlan for this title, this Puzzle Pack will refresh your Unit Resource Materials and Vocabulary Resource Materials sections plus give you additional materials you can substitute into the tests. If you do not already have a complete LitPlan, these pages will give you some supplemental materials to use with your own plan. There are two main groups of materials: one set for unit words (such as characters' names, symbols, places, etc.) and one set for vocabulary words associated with the book.

WORD LIST
There is a word list for both the unit words and the vocabulary words. These lists show you which words are being used in the materials and the clues or definitions being used for those words. You may want to give students a word list with clues/definitions to help them, or you may want students to only have a word list (without clues/definitions) if you want them to work a little harder. Both are available for duplication. The word lists can also be your "calling key" for the bingo games.

FILL IN THE BLANK AND MATCHING
There are 4 each of the fill in the blank and matching worksheets for both the unit and vocabulary words. These pages can be used either as extra worksheets for students or as objective parts of a unit test. They can be done individually if students need extra help or as a whole class activity to review the material covered.

MAGIC SQUARES
The magic squares not only reinforce the material covered but also work on reasoning and math skills. Many teachers have told us that their students really enjoy doing these!

WORD SEARCH PUZZLES
The word search words go in all directions, as indicated on your answer keys. Two of the word search puzzles have the clues listed rather than the words. This makes the puzzle a little more difficult, but it reinforces the material better. Two word search puzzles have words only for students who find the clue puzzles too difficult.

CROSSWORD PUZZLES
Both unit and vocabulary word sections have 4 crossword puzzles.

BINGO CARDS
There are 32 individual bingo cards for the unit words and 32 individual bingo cards for the vocabulary words. You can use your word list as a "call list," calling the words at random and marking them off of your list as you go, or you could use the flash cards by cutting them apart and drawing the words at random from a hat (or box or whatever). To make a better review, you might ask for the definition and spelling of each word as you call it out–or you could call out the definitions and have students tell you the words they need to look for on the puzzle.

JUGGLE LETTERS
The vocabulary juggle letter game is intended to help students learn the spellings of the words. One sheet has the definitions listed on it as an extra help for students who need it or to reinforce the definitions if you choose to do so.

FLASH CARDS
We've included a set of vocabulary flash cards you can duplicate, cut, and fold for your students. Some teachers make a few sets for general use by the class; others make a set for each student. Some teachers duplicate them for each student and have the students cut & fold their own. You can cut out just the words and put them in a hat, have each student pick out one word and write the definition and a sentence for that word. Students then swap words and papers, with the next student adding a sentence of his own under the last one. You can have students swap as many times as you like. Each time the student will read the sentences written prior to his own and then add a sentence. You can cut out the words and definitions separately and play "I Have; Who Has?" Each student in the room draws a word and definition. The first student says, "I have (the name of the word). Who has the definition?" The student with the definition reads it then says, "I have (the name of the vocabulary word she has). Who has the definition?" The round continues until all words and definitions have been given.

Harry Potter & Sorcerer's Stone Unit Word List

No.	Word	Clue/Definition
1.	AGES	Quidditch Through The ____; book Hermione lent Harry
2.	BARON	The Bloody____; Slytherin ghost
3.	DARK	Quirrell's course; Defense Against the ____ Arts
4.	DENTISTS	Hermione's parents' profession
5.	DUDLEY	Harry's cousin
6.	DUMBLEDORE	Headmaster of Hogwarts School
7.	FANG	Hagrid's dog
8.	FILCH	Caretaker of Hogwarts
9.	FLUFFY	Three-headed dog
10.	FOREST	Place off-limits to students; Forbidden____
11.	GRINGOTTS	Wizard bank
12.	GRYFFINDOR	Harry's house at Hogwarts
13.	HAGRID	Keeper of the Keys
14.	HAT	The Sorting____; assigns students to houses at Hogwarts
15.	HEDWIG	Harry's owl
16.	HERMIONE	Girl who applies logic
17.	HOGWARTS	School of Witchcraft and Wizardry
18.	INVISIBILITY	"Just in case" note was left on the ____Cloak
19.	JAMES	Harry's father
20.	JORDAN	Did commentary for the Quidditch match
21.	LILY	Harry's mother
22.	MALFOY	Harry's student rival
23.	MUGGLES	Nonmagic folk
24.	NEVILLE	____Longbottom; won points for standing up to his friends
25.	NICK	Nearly Headless____; resident ghost at Gryffindor House
26.	NORRIS	Mr. Filch's cat
27.	OLLIVANDER	Seller of wands
28.	PEEVES	A poltergeist
29.	PERCY	Prefect at Hogwarts; ____Weasley
30.	PETUNIA	Harry's aunt
31.	QUIDDITCH	Wizard game
32.	ROWLING	Author of the Harry Potter books
33.	SCABBERS	Ron's rat
34.	SEEKER	Harry's role in Quidditch
35.	SLYTHERIN	Voldemort's house at Hogwarts
36.	SNAPE	Master of Potions
37.	SNITCH	Ball the Seeker had to catch; The Golden____
38.	SPROUT	Herbology professor
39.	TREVOR	Neville's toad
40.	TWINS	Fred and George were ____
41.	VERNON	Harry's uncle
42.	VOLDEMORT	Wizard gone bad
43.	WEASLEY	Harry's close, red-haired friend

Copyrighted

Harry Potter Sorcerer's Stone Fill In The Blank 1

1. A poltergeist
2. Prefect at Hogwarts; ____Weasley
3. Did commentary for the Quidditch match
4. Three-headed dog
5. School of Witchcraft and Wizardry
6. The Sorting____; assigns students to houses at Hogwarts
7. ____Longbottom; won points for standing up to his friends
8. Quirrell's course; Defense Against the ____ Arts
9. Harry's role in Quidditch
10. Harry's close, red-haired friend
11. Harry's house at Hogwarts
12. Hagrid's dog
13. Master of Potions
14. Wizard game
15. Ron's rat
16. "Just in case" note was left on the ____Cloak
17. Caretaker of Hogwarts
18. Herbology professor
19. Harry's cousin
20. Hermione's parents' profession

Harry Potter Sorcerer's Stone Fill In The Blank 1 Answer Key

PEEVES	1. A poltergeist
PERCY	2. Prefect at Hogwarts; ____Weasley
JORDAN	3. Did commentary for the Quidditch match
FLUFFY	4. Three-headed dog
HOGWARTS	5. School of Witchcraft and Wizardry
HAT	6. The Sorting____; assigns students to houses at Hogwarts
NEVILLE	7. ____Longbottom; won points for standing up to his friends
DARK	8. Quirrell's course; Defense Against the ____ Arts
SEEKER	9. Harry's role in Quidditch
WEASLEY	10. Harry's close, red-haired friend
GRYFFINDOR	11. Harry's house at Hogwarts
FANG	12. Hagrid's dog
SNAPE	13. Master of Potions
QUIDDITCH	14. Wizard game
SCABBERS	15. Ron's rat
INVISIBILITY	16. "Just in case" note was left on the ____Cloak
FILCH	17. Caretaker of Hogwarts
SPROUT	18. Herbology professor
DUDLEY	19. Harry's cousin
DENTISTS	20. Hermione's parents' profession

Harry Potter Sorcerer's Stone Fill In The Blank 2

1. Nearly Headless____; resident ghost at Gryffindor House
2. Harry's cousin
3. Fred and George were ____
4. Wizard gone bad
5. Harry's house at Hogwarts
6. Neville's toad
7. Hermione's parents' profession
8. Headmaster of Hogwarts School
9. Master of Potions
10. Hagrid's dog
11. Author of the Harry Potter books
12. Place off-limits to students; Forbidden____
13. Harry's role in Quidditch
14. Ron's rat
15. Keeper of the Keys
16. Quidditch Through The ____; book Hermione lent Harry
17. Herbology professor
18. Harry's owl
19. Mr. Filch's cat
20. Harry's close, red-haired friend

Harry Potter Sorcerer's Stone Fill In The Blank 2 Answer Key

NICK	1. Nearly Headless____; resident ghost at Gryffindor House
DUDLEY	2. Harry's cousin
TWINS	3. Fred and George were ____
VOLDEMORT	4. Wizard gone bad
GRYFFINDOR	5. Harry's house at Hogwarts
TREVOR	6. Neville's toad
DENTISTS	7. Hermione's parents' profession
DUMBLEDORE	8. Headmaster of Hogwarts School
SNAPE	9. Master of Potions
FANG	10. Hagrid's dog
ROWLING	11. Author of the Harry Potter books
FOREST	12. Place off-limits to students; Forbidden____
SEEKER	13. Harry's role in Quidditch
SCABBERS	14. Ron's rat
HAGRID	15. Keeper of the Keys
AGES	16. Quidditch Through The ____; book Hermione lent Harry
SPROUT	17. Herbology professor
HEDWIG	18. Harry's owl
NORRIS	19. Mr. Filch's cat
WEASLEY	20. Harry's close, red-haired friend

Harry Potter Sorcerer's Stone Fill In The Blank 3

_____ 1. Master of Potions

_____ 2. Neville's toad

_____ 3. "Just in case" note was left on the ____Cloak

_____ 4. Ball the Seeker had to catch; The Golden____

_____ 5. Fred and George were ____

_____ 6. Harry's mother

_____ 7. Wizard bank

_____ 8. The Sorting____; assigns students to houses at Hogwarts

_____ 9. Place off-limits to students; Forbidden____

_____ 10. Caretaker of Hogwarts

_____ 11. Ron's rat

_____ 12. Wizard game

_____ 13. A poltergeist

_____ 14. Harry's father

_____ 15. Voldemort's house at Hogwarts

_____ 16. Quirrell's course; Defense Against the ____ Arts

_____ 17. Quidditch Through The ____; book Hermione lent Harry

_____ 18. Mr. Filch's cat

_____ 19. Girl who applies logic

_____ 20. Harry's uncle

Harry Potter Sorcerer's Stone Fill In The Blank 3 Answer Key

SNAPE	1. Master of Potions
TREVOR	2. Neville's toad
INVISIBILITY	3. "Just in case" note was left on the ____Cloak
SNITCH	4. Ball the Seeker had to catch; The Golden____
TWINS	5. Fred and George were ____
LILY	6. Harry's mother
GRINGOTTS	7. Wizard bank
HAT	8. The Sorting____; assigns students to houses at Hogwarts
FOREST	9. Place off-limits to students; Forbidden____
FILCH	10. Caretaker of Hogwarts
SCABBERS	11. Ron's rat
QUIDDITCH	12. Wizard game
PEEVES	13. A poltergeist
JAMES	14. Harry's father
SLYTHERIN	15. Voldemort's house at Hogwarts
DARK	16. Quirrell's course; Defense Against the ____ Arts
AGES	17. Quidditch Through The ____; book Hermione lent Harry
NORRIS	18. Mr. Filch's cat
HERMIONE	19. Girl who applies logic
VERNON	20. Harry's uncle

Harry Potter Sorcerer's Stone Fill In The Blank 4

_____ 1. Harry's father
_____ 2. The Sorting____; assigns students to houses at Hogwarts
_____ 3. Prefect at Hogwarts;____Weasley
_____ 4. ____Longbottom; won points for standing up to his friends
_____ 5. Harry's uncle
_____ 6. A poltergeist
_____ 7. Master of Potions
_____ 8. Ron's rat
_____ 9. Ball the Seeker had to catch; The Golden____
_____ 10. Caretaker of Hogwarts
_____ 11. Harry's cousin
_____ 12. Seller of wands
_____ 13. Quidditch Through The ____; book Hermione lent Harry
_____ 14. "Just in case" note was left on the ____Cloak
_____ 15. Mr. Filch's cat
_____ 16. Herbology professor
_____ 17. Harry's close, red-haired friend
_____ 18. Harry's student rival
_____ 19. Voldemort's house at Hogwarts
_____ 20. Three-headed dog

Harry Potter Sorcerer's Stone Fill In The Blank 4 Answer Key

JAMES	1. Harry's father
HAT	2. The Sorting____; assigns students to houses at Hogwarts
PERCY	3. Prefect at Hogwarts;____Weasley
NEVILLE	4. ____Longbottom; won points for standing up to his friends
VERNON	5. Harry's uncle
PEEVES	6. A poltergeist
SNAPE	7. Master of Potions
SCABBERS	8. Ron's rat
SNITCH	9. Ball the Seeker had to catch; The Golden____
FILCH	10. Caretaker of Hogwarts
DUDLEY	11. Harry's cousin
OLLIVANDER	12. Seller of wands
AGES	13. Quidditch Through The ____; book Hermione lent Harry
INVISIBILITY	14. "Just in case" note was left on the ____Cloak
NORRIS	15. Mr. Filch's cat
SPROUT	16. Herbology professor
WEASLEY	17. Harry's close, red-haired friend
MALFOY	18. Harry's student rival
SLYTHERIN	19. Voldemort's house at Hogwarts
FLUFFY	20. Three-headed dog

Harry Potter Sorcerer's Stone Matching 1

___ 1. FILCH   A. The Sorting____; assigns students to houses at Hogwarts
___ 2. FOREST   B. Harry's student rival
___ 3. HAT   C. Did commentary for the Quidditch match
___ 4. NICK   D. Wizard game
___ 5. MALFOY   E. Prefect at Hogwarts;____Weasley
___ 6. HERMIONE   F. Place off-limits to students; Forbidden____
___ 7. PETUNIA   G. Quidditch Through The ____; book Hermione lent Harry
___ 8. TREVOR   H. Quirrell's course; Defense Against the ____ Arts
___ 9. MUGGLES   I. Keeper of the Keys
___10. JAMES   J. Harry's father
___11. GRINGOTTS   K. Harry's mother
___12. PEEVES   L. A poltergeist
___13. JORDAN   M. Hermione's parents' profession
___14. PERCY   N. Nonmagic folk
___15. VOLDEMORT   O. Nearly Headless____; resident ghost at Gryffindor House
___16. GRYFFINDOR   P. Headmaster of Hogwarts School
___17. DARK   Q. Harry's house at Hogwarts
___18. AGES   R. Harry's aunt
___19. LILY   S. Voldemort's house at Hogwarts
___20. HAGRID   T. Wizard gone bad
___21. DENTISTS   U. Harry's cousin
___22. QUIDDITCH   V. Caretaker of Hogwarts
___23. DUMBLEDORE   W. Wizard bank
___24. DUDLEY   X. Girl who applies logic
___25. SLYTHERIN   Y. Neville's toad

Harry Potter Sorcerer's Stone Matching 1 Answer Key

V - 1. FILCH	A.	The Sorting____; assigns students to houses at Hogwarts
F - 2. FOREST	B.	Harry's student rival
A - 3. HAT	C.	Did commentary for the Quidditch match
O - 4. NICK	D.	Wizard game
B - 5. MALFOY	E.	Prefect at Hogwarts;____Weasley
X - 6. HERMIONE	F.	Place off-limits to students; Forbidden____
R - 7. PETUNIA	G.	Quidditch Through The ____; book Hermione lent Harry
Y - 8. TREVOR	H.	Quirrell's course; Defense Against the ____ Arts
N - 9. MUGGLES	I.	Keeper of the Keys
J - 10. JAMES	J.	Harry's father
W - 11. GRINGOTTS	K.	Harry's mother
L - 12. PEEVES	L.	A poltergeist
C - 13. JORDAN	M.	Hermione's parents' profession
E - 14. PERCY	N.	Nonmagic folk
T - 15. VOLDEMORT	O.	Nearly Headless____; resident ghost at Gryffindor House
Q - 16. GRYFFINDOR	P.	Headmaster of Hogwarts School
H - 17. DARK	Q.	Harry's house at Hogwarts
G - 18. AGES	R.	Harry's aunt
K - 19. LILY	S.	Voldemort's house at Hogwarts
I - 20. HAGRID	T.	Wizard gone bad
M - 21. DENTISTS	U.	Harry's cousin
D - 22. QUIDDITCH	V.	Caretaker of Hogwarts
P - 23. DUMBLEDORE	W.	Wizard bank
U - 24. DUDLEY	X.	Girl who applies logic
S - 25. SLYTHERIN	Y.	Neville's toad

Harry Potter Sorcerer's Stone Matching 2

___ 1. WEASLEY   A. Harry's house at Hogwarts
___ 2. FILCH   B. Fred and George were ____
___ 3. JORDAN   C. Quirrell's course; Defense Against the ____ Arts
___ 4. BARON   D. Nearly Headless____; resident ghost at Gryffindor House
___ 5. DARK   E. Nonmagic folk
___ 6. PETUNIA   F. Harry's mother
___ 7. TWINS   G. Harry's cousin
___ 8. JAMES   H. The Bloody____; Slytherin ghost
___ 9. NEVILLE   I. Harry's student rival
___10. GRYFFINDOR   J. Harry's owl
___11. MALFOY   K. Hermione's parents' profession
___12. DUDLEY   L. Wizard game
___13. QUIDDITCH   M. Ball the Seeker had to catch; The Golden____
___14. GRINGOTTS   N. Caretaker of Hogwarts
___15. HAT   O. Harry's father
___16. NORRIS   P. Did commentary for the Quidditch match
___17. NICK   Q. Wizard bank
___18. SNITCH   R. ____Longbottom; won points for standing up to his friends
___19. FLUFFY   S. Three-headed dog
___20. DENTISTS   T. Harry's close, red-haired friend
___21. SPROUT   U. Harry's aunt
___22. MUGGLES   V. Quidditch Through The ____; book Hermione lent Harry
___23. AGES   W. Mr. Filch's cat
___24. HEDWIG   X. The Sorting____; assigns students to houses at Hogwarts
___25. LILY   Y. Herbology professor

Harry Potter Sorcerer's Stone Matching 2 Answer Key

T - 1.	WEASLEY	A.	Harry's house at Hogwarts
N - 2.	FILCH	B.	Fred and George were ____
P - 3.	JORDAN	C.	Quirrell's course; Defense Against the ____ Arts
H - 4.	BARON	D.	Nearly Headless____; resident ghost at Gryffindor House
C - 5.	DARK	E.	Nonmagic folk
U - 6.	PETUNIA	F.	Harry's mother
B - 7.	TWINS	G.	Harry's cousin
O - 8.	JAMES	H.	The Bloody____; Slytherin ghost
R - 9.	NEVILLE	I.	Harry's student rival
A - 10.	GRYFFINDOR	J.	Harry's owl
I - 11.	MALFOY	K.	Hermione's parents' profession
G - 12.	DUDLEY	L.	Wizard game
L - 13.	QUIDDITCH	M.	Ball the Seeker had to catch; The Golden____
Q - 14.	GRINGOTTS	N.	Caretaker of Hogwarts
X - 15.	HAT	O.	Harry's father
W - 16.	NORRIS	P.	Did commentary for the Quidditch match
D - 17.	NICK	Q.	Wizard bank
M - 18.	SNITCH	R.	____Longbottom; won points for standing up to his friends
S - 19.	FLUFFY	S.	Three-headed dog
K - 20.	DENTISTS	T.	Harry's close, red-haired friend
Y - 21.	SPROUT	U.	Harry's aunt
E - 22.	MUGGLES	V.	Quidditch Through The ____; book Hermione lent Harry
V - 23.	AGES	W.	Mr. Filch's cat
J - 24.	HEDWIG	X.	The Sorting____; assigns students to houses at Hogwarts
F - 25.	LILY	Y.	Herbology professor

Harry Potter Sorcerer's Stone Matching 3

___ 1. FLUFFY
___ 2. SNAPE
___ 3. FOREST
___ 4. SEEKER
___ 5. NICK
___ 6. LILY
___ 7. SNITCH
___ 8. DUDLEY
___ 9. MALFOY
___ 10. FANG
___ 11. HAGRID
___ 12. INVISIBILITY
___ 13. VERNON
___ 14. AGES
___ 15. JORDAN
___ 16. VOLDEMORT
___ 17. SPROUT
___ 18. BARON
___ 19. TREVOR
___ 20. QUIDDITCH
___ 21. NEVILLE
___ 22. DUMBLEDORE
___ 23. SLYTHERIN
___ 24. HERMIONE
___ 25. OLLIVANDER

A. Herbology professor
B. "Just in case" note was left on the ____Cloak
C. Keeper of the Keys
D. Wizard game
E. Nearly Headless____; resident ghost at Gryffindor House
F. Ball the Seeker had to catch; The Golden____
G. Wizard gone bad
H. Harry's student rival
I. Neville's toad
J. Harry's uncle
K. Harry's cousin
L. Headmaster of Hogwarts School
M. Quidditch Through The ____; book Hermione lent Harry
N. Harry's mother
O. Master of Potions
P. Place off-limits to students; Forbidden____
Q. Hagrid's dog
R. Girl who applies logic
S. Did commentary for the Quidditch match
T. Harry's role in Quidditch
U. Three-headed dog
V. Seller of wands
W. ____Longbottom; won points for standing up to his friends
X. The Bloody____; Slytherin ghost
Y. Voldemort's house at Hogwarts

Harry Potter Sorcerer's Stone Matching 3 Answer Key

U - 1.	FLUFFY	A. Herbology professor
O - 2.	SNAPE	B. "Just in case" note was left on the ____Cloak
P - 3.	FOREST	C. Keeper of the Keys
T - 4.	SEEKER	D. Wizard game
E - 5.	NICK	E. Nearly Headless____; resident ghost at Gryffindor House
N - 6.	LILY	F. Ball the Seeker had to catch; The Golden____
F - 7.	SNITCH	G. Wizard gone bad
K - 8.	DUDLEY	H. Harry's student rival
H - 9.	MALFOY	I. Neville's toad
Q -10.	FANG	J. Harry's uncle
C -11.	HAGRID	K. Harry's cousin
B -12.	INVISIBILITY	L. Headmaster of Hogwarts School
J -13.	VERNON	M. Quidditch Through The ____; book Hermione lent Harry
M -14.	AGES	N. Harry's mother
S -15.	JORDAN	O. Master of Potions
G -16.	VOLDEMORT	P. Place off-limits to students; Forbidden____
A -17.	SPROUT	Q. Hagrid's dog
X -18.	BARON	R. Girl who applies logic
I -19.	TREVOR	S. Did commentary for the Quidditch match
D -20.	QUIDDITCH	T. Harry's role in Quidditch
W -21.	NEVILLE	U. Three-headed dog
L -22.	DUMBLEDORE	V. Seller of wands
Y -23.	SLYTHERIN	W. ____Longbottom; won points for standing up to his friends
R -24.	HERMIONE	X. The Bloody____; Slytherin ghost
V -25.	OLLIVANDER	Y. Voldemort's house at Hogwarts

Harry Potter Sorcerer's Stone Matching 4

___ 1. DARK   A. Ron's rat
___ 2. MUGGLES   B. Neville's toad
___ 3. HERMIONE   C. Harry's father
___ 4. NEVILLE   D. Harry's role in Quidditch
___ 5. MALFOY   E. Harry's student rival
___ 6. HAT   F. Quirrell's course; Defense Against the ____ Arts
___ 7. PETUNIA   G. Wizard bank
___ 8. NICK   H. Hermione's parents' profession
___ 9. GRINGOTTS   I. ____Longbottom; won points for standing up to his friends
___10. SCABBERS   J. The Sorting____; assigns students to houses at Hogwarts
___11. GRYFFINDOR   K. Nonmagic folk
___12. AGES   L. Three-headed dog
___13. SEEKER   M. Girl who applies logic
___14. FOREST   N. Ball the Seeker had to catch; The Golden____
___15. LILY   O. Harry's house at Hogwarts
___16. WEASLEY   P. Harry's mother
___17. TREVOR   Q. Harry's close, red-haired friend
___18. FLUFFY   R. Seller of wands
___19. OLLIVANDER   S. Nearly Headless____; resident ghost at Gryffindor House
___20. JAMES   T. Harry's aunt
___21. SNITCH   U. Place off-limits to students; Forbidden____
___22. HAGRID   V. Master of Potions
___23. DENTISTS   W. Keeper of the Keys
___24. SNAPE   X. Author of the Harry Potter books
___25. ROWLING   Y. Quidditch Through The ____; book Hermione lent Harry

Harry Potter Sorcerer's Stone Matching 4 Answer Key

F - 1. DARK	A. Ron's rat
K - 2. MUGGLES	B. Neville's toad
M - 3. HERMIONE	C. Harry's father
I - 4. NEVILLE	D. Harry's role in Quidditch
E - 5. MALFOY	E. Harry's student rival
J - 6. HAT	F. Quirrell's course; Defense Against the ____ Arts
T - 7. PETUNIA	G. Wizard bank
S - 8. NICK	H. Hermione's parents' profession
G - 9. GRINGOTTS	I. ____Longbottom; won points for standing up to his friends
A - 10. SCABBERS	J. The Sorting____; assigns students to houses at Hogwarts
O - 11. GRYFFINDOR	K. Nonmagic folk
Y - 12. AGES	L. Three-headed dog
D - 13. SEEKER	M. Girl who applies logic
U - 14. FOREST	N. Ball the Seeker had to catch; The Golden____
P - 15. LILY	O. Harry's house at Hogwarts
Q - 16. WEASLEY	P. Harry's mother
B - 17. TREVOR	Q. Harry's close, red-haired friend
L - 18. FLUFFY	R. Seller of wands
R - 19. OLLIVANDER	S. Nearly Headless____; resident ghost at Gryffindor House
C - 20. JAMES	T. Harry's aunt
N - 21. SNITCH	U. Place off-limits to students; Forbidden____
W - 22. HAGRID	V. Master of Potions
H - 23. DENTISTS	W. Keeper of the Keys
V - 24. SNAPE	X. Author of the Harry Potter books
X - 25. ROWLING	Y. Quidditch Through The ____; book Hermione lent Harry

Harry Potter Sorcerer's Stone Magic Squares 1

Match the definition with the vocabulary word. Put your answers in the magic squares below. When your answers are correct, all columns and rows will add to the same number.

A. DUMBLEDORE   E. MALFOY   I. FLUFFY   M. HAT
B. QUIDDITCH   F. ROWLING   J. HEDWIG   N. FOREST
C. WEASLEY   G. HERMIONE   K. VERNON   O. PERCY
D. SEEKER   H. DUDLEY   L. PEEVES   P. NEVILLE

1. Place off-limits to students; Forbidden____
2. Girl who applies logic
3. A poltergeist
4. Headmaster of Hogwarts School
5. Harry's uncle
6. Wizard game
7. The Sorting____; assigns students to houses at Hogwarts
8. Harry's cousin
9. Harry's student rival
10. ____Longbottom; won points for standing up to his friends
11. Harry's close, red-haired friend
12. Harry's owl
13. Harry's role in Quidditch
14. Three-headed dog
15. Author of the Harry Potter books
16. Prefect at Hogwarts;____Weasley

A=	B=	C=	D=
E=	F=	G=	H=
I=	J=	K=	L=
M=	N=	O=	P=

Harry Potter Sorcerer's Stone Magic Squares 1 Answer Key

Match the definition with the vocabulary word. Put your answers in the magic squares below. When your answers are correct, all columns and rows will add to the same number.

A. DUMBLEDORE E. MALFOY   I. FLUFFY   M. HAT
B. QUIDDITCH   F. ROWLING   J. HEDWIG   N. FOREST
C. WEASLEY   G. HERMIONE   K. VERNON   O. PERCY
D. SEEKER   H. DUDLEY   L. PEEVES   P. NEVILLE

1. Place off-limits to students; Forbidden____
2. Girl who applies logic
3. A poltergeist
4. Headmaster of Hogwarts School
5. Harry's uncle
6. Wizard game
7. The Sorting____; assigns students to houses at Hogwarts
8. Harry's cousin
9. Harry's student rival
10. ____Longbottom; won points for standing up to his friends
11. Harry's close, red-haired friend
12. Harry's owl
13. Harry's role in Quidditch
14. Three-headed dog
15. Author of the Harry Potter books
16. Prefect at Hogwarts;____Weasley

A=4	B=6	C=11	D=13
E=9	F=15	G=2	H=8
I=14	J=12	K=5	L=3
M=7	N=1	O=16	P=10

Copyrighted

Harry Potter Sorcerer's Stone Magic Squares 2

Match the definition with the vocabulary word. Put your answers in the magic squares below. When your answers are correct, all columns and rows will add to the same number.

A. HERMIONE E. SCABBERS I. INVISIBILITY M. DUDLEY
B. HEDWIG F. LILY J. DUMBLEDORE N. FOREST
C. SLYTHERIN G. JORDAN K. TREVOR O. FANG
D. ROWLING H. GRYFFINDOR L. SNAPE P. JAMES

1. Harry's mother
2. "Just in case" note was left on the ___Cloak
3. Hagrid's dog
4. Author of the Harry Potter books
5. Harry's cousin
6. Harry's owl
7. Harry's house at Hogwarts
8. Neville's toad
9. Voldemort's house at Hogwarts
10. Harry's father
11. Headmaster of Hogwarts School
12. Ron's rat
13. Master of Potions
14. Did commentary for the Quidditch match
15. Girl who applies logic
16. Place off-limits to students; Forbidden___

A=	B=	C=	D=
E=	F=	G=	H=
I=	J=	K=	L=
M=	N=	O=	P=

23
Copyrighted

Harry Potter Sorcerer's Stone Magic Squares 2 Answer Key

Match the definition with the vocabulary word. Put your answers in the magic squares below. When your answers are correct, all columns and rows will add to the same number.

A. HERMIONE
B. HEDWIG
C. SLYTHERIN
D. ROWLING
E. SCABBERS
F. LILY
G. JORDAN
H. GRYFFINDOR
I. INVISIBILITY
J. DUMBLEDORE
K. TREVOR
L. SNAPE
M. DUDLEY
N. FOREST
O. FANG
P. JAMES

1. Harry's mother
2. "Just in case" note was left on the __Cloak
3. Hagrid's dog
4. Author of the Harry Potter books
5. Harry's cousin
6. Harry's owl
7. Harry's house at Hogwarts
8. Neville's toad
9. Voldemort's house at Hogwarts
10. Harry's father
11. Headmaster of Hogwarts School
12. Ron's rat
13. Master of Potions
14. Did commentary for the Quidditch match
15. Girl who applies logic
16. Place off-limits to students; Forbidden____

A=15	B=6	C=9	D=4
E=12	F=1	G=14	H=7
I=2	J=11	K=8	L=13
M=5	N=16	O=3	P=10

Harry Potter Sorcerer's Stone Magic Squares 3

Match the definition with the vocabulary word. Put your answers in the magic squares below. When your answers are correct, all columns and rows will add to the same number.

A. FOREST
B. VOLDEMORT
C. ROWLING
D. FANG
E. SCABBERS
F. PETUNIA
G. DARK
H. TWINS
I. JAMES
J. SPROUT
K. NEVILLE
L. HOGWARTS
M. NICK
N. TREVOR
O. HAT
P. LILY

1. Author of the Harry Potter books
2. Herbology professor
3. Harry's aunt
4. The Sorting____; assigns students to houses at Hogwarts
5. Harry's mother
6. Ron's rat
7. Harry's father
8. Hagrid's dog
9. Nearly Headless____; resident ghost at Gryffindor House
10. Fred and George were ____
11. School of Witchcraft and Wizardry
12. Place off-limits to students; Forbidden____
13. Wizard gone bad
14. ____Longbottom; won points for standing up to his friends
15. Quirrell's course; Defense Against the ____ Arts
16. Neville's toad

A=	B=	C=	D=
E=	F=	G=	H=
I=	J=	K=	L=
M=	N=	O=	P=

25
Copyrighted

Harry Potter Sorcerer's Stone Magic Squares 3 Answer Key

Match the definition with the vocabulary word. Put your answers in the magic squares below. When your answers are correct, all columns and rows will add to the same number.

A. FOREST
B. VOLDEMORT
C. ROWLING
D. FANG
E. SCABBERS
F. PETUNIA
G. DARK
H. TWINS
I. JAMES
J. SPROUT
K. NEVILLE
L. HOGWARTS
M. NICK
N. TREVOR
O. HAT
P. LILY

1. Author of the Harry Potter books
2. Herbology professor
3. Harry's aunt
4. The Sorting____; assigns students to houses at Hogwarts
5. Harry's mother
6. Ron's rat
7. Harry's father
8. Hagrid's dog
9. Nearly Headless____; resident ghost at Gryffindor House
10. Fred and George were ____
11. School of Witchcraft and Wizardry
12. Place off-limits to students; Forbidden____
13. Wizard gone bad
14. ____Longbottom; won points for standing up to his friends
15. Quirrell's course; Defense Against the ____ Arts
16. Neville's toad

A=12	B=13	C=1	D=8
E=6	F=3	G=15	H=10
I=7	J=2	K=14	L=11
M=9	N=16	O=4	P=5

Harry Potter Sorcerer's Stone Magic Squares 4

Match the definition with the vocabulary word. Put your answers in the magic squares below. When your answers are correct, all columns and rows will add to the same number.

A. BARON   E. TREVOR   I. SLYTHERIN   M. HAT
B. NEVILLE   F. DUMBLEDORE   J. TWINS   N. AGES
C. NICK   G. PEEVES   K. HAGRID   O. DARK
D. VERNON   H. JAMES   L. DENTISTS   P. SNAPE

1. ____Longbottom; won points for standing up to his friends
2. A poltergeist
3. Keeper of the Keys
4. Quidditch Through The ____; book Hermione lent Harry
5. The Sorting____; assigns students to houses at Hogwarts
6. Hermione's parents' profession
7. Harry's father
8. The Bloody____; Slytherin ghost
9. Master of Potions
10. Voldemort's house at Hogwarts
11. Neville's toad
12. Harry's uncle
13. Nearly Headless____; resident ghost at Gryffindor House
14. Headmaster of Hogwarts School
15. Fred and George were ____
16. Quirrell's course; Defense Against the ____ Arts

A=	B=	C=	D=
E=	F=	G=	H=
I=	J=	K=	L=
M=	N=	O=	P=

27
Copyrighted

Harry Potter Sorcerer's Stone Magic Squares 4 Answer Key

Match the definition with the vocabulary word. Put your answers in the magic squares below. When your answers are correct, all columns and rows will add to the same number.

A. BARON
B. NEVILLE
C. NICK
D. VERNON
E. TREVOR
F. DUMBLEDORE
G. PEEVES
H. JAMES
I. SLYTHERIN
J. TWINS
K. HAGRID
L. DENTISTS
M. HAT
N. AGES
O. DARK
P. SNAPE

1. ____Longbottom; won points for standing up to his friends
2. A poltergeist
3. Keeper of the Keys
4. Quidditch Through The ____; book Hermione lent Harry
5. The Sorting____; assigns students to houses at Hogwarts
6. Hermione's parents' profession
7. Harry's father
8. The Bloody____; Slytherin ghost
9. Master of Potions
10. Voldemort's house at Hogwarts
11. Neville's toad
12. Harry's uncle
13. Nearly Headless____; resident ghost at Gryffindor House
14. Headmaster of Hogwarts School
15. Fred and George were ____
16. Quirrell's course; Defense Against the ____ Arts

A=8	B=1	C=13	D=12
E=11	F=14	G=2	H=7
I=10	J=15	K=3	L=6
M=5	N=4	O=16	P=9

Harry Potter Sorcerer's Stone Word Search 1

```
P H O G W A R T S T G G V V D B G D S S
H J T N S J D P T U C K Z J Y B O U I F
D V K B L S A G Z O Q P Q S Y D L D R N
P K T P S R J M S R M C W K J I L L R K
E Z D Y E T F M E P K Y S M R R I E O V
E W F P D G R M W S B A R O N G V Y N K
V F A N C A Q S R H J G V S N A A O H T
E N L Y Y C R E N G O E N A X H N N E V
S N I T C H B K E R R B F P X R D I R V
G M S M Z B M X V T D Y Y M E W E C M J
R A S L A T D Q I Y A P F V U R R K I R
I L V C Y F F U L F N T I F M G C M O R
N F S O W T Y T L T S B L H I G G Y N M
G O E Q L L H S E E Y W C J E N L L E D
O Y E F I D K E R C T A H N P D D Y E V
T D K L W E E O R F L T P G E P W O Z S
T D E H E N F M H I S W N V T J S I R K
S L R H A T A J O T N I D R U V T N G N
P D L W S I D G B R L N B R N B Y K H G
K K W C L S G M E W T S X Z I J Z H K M
R L L Y E T N Z O S S S M N A M P X G X
L D P F Y S E R O D E L B M U D P Z Z V
```

A poltergeist (6)
Author of the Harry Potter books (7)
Ball the Seeker had to catch; The Golden____ (6)
Caretaker of Hogwarts (5)
Did commentary for the Quidditch match (6)
Fred and George were ____ (5)
Girl who applies logic (8)
Hagrid's dog (4)
Harry's aunt (7)
Harry's close, red-haired friend (7)
Harry's cousin (6)
Harry's father (5)
Harry's house at Hogwarts (10)
Harry's mother (4)
Harry's owl (6)
Harry's role in Quidditch (6)
Harry's student rival (6)
Harry's uncle (6)
Headmaster of Hogwarts School (10)
Herbology professor (6)
Hermione's parents' profession (8)
Keeper of the Keys (6)
Master of Potions (5)
Mr. Filch's cat (6)
Nearly Headless____; resident ghost at Gryffindor House (4)
Neville's toad (6)
Nonmagic folk (7)
Place off-limits to students; Forbidden____ (6)
Prefect at Hogwarts;____Weasley (5)
Quidditch Through The ____; book Hermione lent Harry (4)
Quirrell's course; Defense Against the ____ Arts (4)
Ron's rat (8)
School of Witchcraft and Wizardry (8)
Seller of wands (10)
The Bloody____; Slytherin ghost (5)
The Sorting____; assigns students to houses at Hogwarts (3)
Three-headed dog (6)
Voldemort's house at Hogwarts (9)
Wizard bank (9)
Wizard gone bad (9)
____Longbottom; won points for standing up to his friends (7)

Harry Potter Sorcerer's Stone Word Search 1 Answer Key

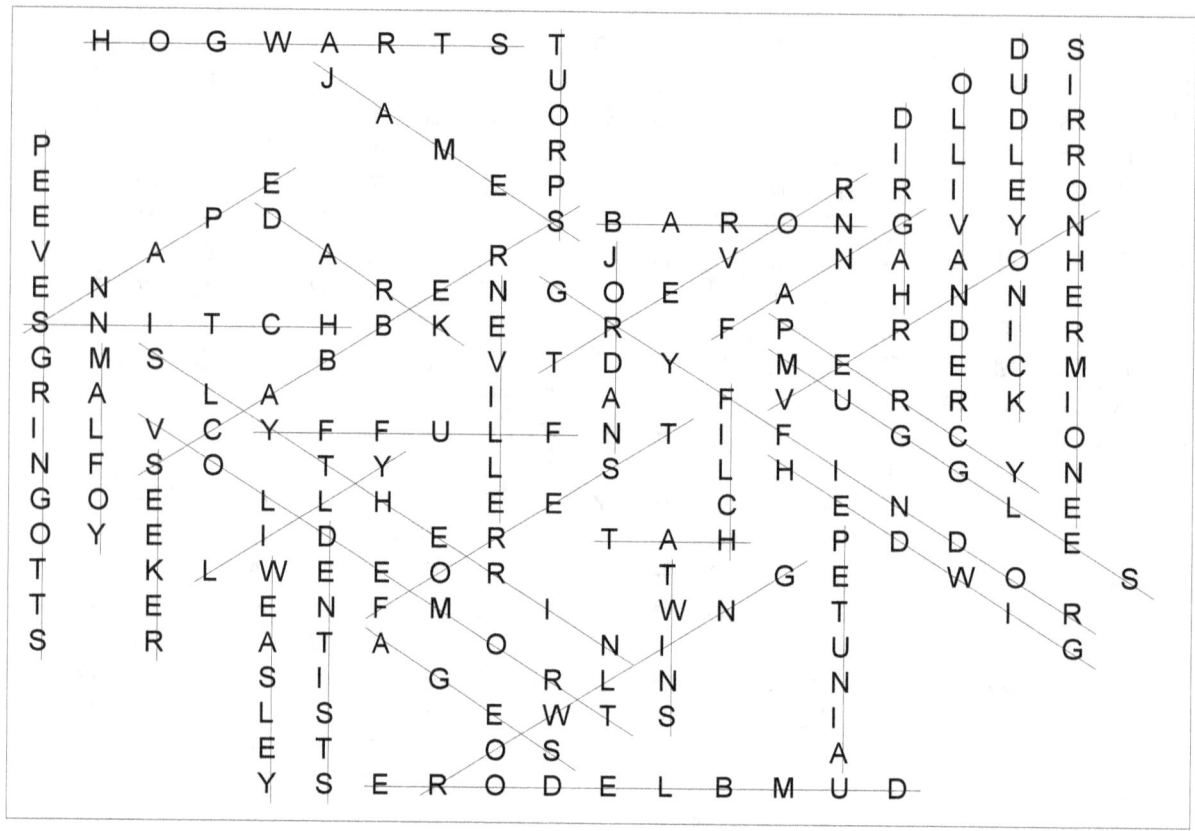

A poltergeist (6)
Author of the Harry Potter books (7)
Ball the Seeker had to catch; The Golden____ (6)
Caretaker of Hogwarts (5)
Did commentary for the Quidditch match (6)
Fred and George were ____ (5)
Girl who applies logic (8)
Hagrid's dog (4)
Harry's aunt (7)
Harry's close, red-haired friend (7)
Harry's cousin (6)
Harry's father (5)
Harry's house at Hogwarts (10)
Harry's mother (4)
Harry's owl (6)
Harry's role in Quidditch (6)
Harry's student rival (6)
Harry's uncle (6)
Headmaster of Hogwarts School (10)
Herbology professor (6)
Hermione's parents' profession (8)
Keeper of the Keys (6)
Master of Potions (5)

Mr. Filch's cat (6)
Nearly Headless____; resident ghost at Gryffindor House (4)
Neville's toad (6)
Nonmagic folk (7)
Place off-limits to students; Forbidden____ (6)
Prefect at Hogwarts;____Weasley (5)
Quidditch Through The ____; book Hermione lent Harry (4)
Quirrell's course; Defense Against the ____ Arts (4)
Ron's rat (8)
School of Witchcraft and Wizardry (8)
Seller of wands (10)
The Bloody____; Slytherin ghost (5)
The Sorting____; assigns students to houses at Hogwarts (3)
Three-headed dog (6)
Voldemort's house at Hogwarts (9)
Wizard bank (9)
Wizard gone bad (9)
____Longbottom; won points for standing up to his friends (7)

Harry Potter Sorcerer's Stone Word Search 2

```
N K R M B H A X Z H Q N Y V D X T F X F
W B K T U P E G H H T I E E L X D V E R
N X K S E G N D E K M R L R Y J P O L L
J A M E S A G T W S R E D N A V I L L O
B G V R F M A L N I R H U O I G Z D I C
S E V O B H G I E O G T D N F C S E V G
S P R F D A W N D S M Y P H J V K M E Y
D A R K T R E N H A L E C A R H O N F
V F N O F Y L O F S L S T Y P G E R Z Q
D N Q H U B N H N L F R U E R L R T D P
H P Q Z M T O C O N O Y N L X F M I V Y
Y F F U L F R T C G Y W I S V M I Q D F
K K D J M O R B X T W L A A G C O L Z L
D G S V W Y I H K N Y A N E X D N Q C D
K R S L N H S X A T F B R W F W E F S H
N I I Q U I D D I T C H S T S I T N E D
B N X J B V R X M K Q C T E S N D H Y F
G G K B F O T Y C J S T H R E D A F G Z
N O Z F J X C W R P R I B M E K P P Q L
Q T Y Q Q R X D R W S N W Q L V E B E Z
L T K M E V L B T T K S K N J G O R Y R
X S T P S C A B B E R S L C R W C R R T
```

A poltergeist (6)
Author of the Harry Potter books (7)
Ball the Seeker had to catch; The Golden____ (6)
Caretaker of Hogwarts (5)
Did commentary for the Quidditch match (6)
Fred and George were ____ (5)
Girl who applies logic (8)
Hagrid's dog (4)
Harry's aunt (7)
Harry's close, red-haired friend (7)
Harry's cousin (6)
Harry's father (5)
Harry's mother (4)
Harry's owl (6)
Harry's role in Quidditch (6)
Harry's student rival (6)
Harry's uncle (6)
Headmaster of Hogwarts School (10)
Herbology professor (6)
Hermione's parents' profession (8)
Keeper of the Keys (6)
Master of Potions (5)
Mr. Filch's cat (6)

Nearly Headless____; resident ghost at Gryffindor House (4)
Neville's toad (6)
Nonmagic folk (7)
Place off-limits to students; Forbidden____ (6)
Prefect at Hogwarts;____Weasley (5)
Quidditch Through The ____; book Hermione lent Harry (4)
Quirrell's course; Defense Against the ____ Arts (4)
Ron's rat (8)
School of Witchcraft and Wizardry (8)
Seller of wands (10)
The Bloody____; Slytherin ghost (5)
The Sorting____; assigns students to houses at Hogwarts (3)
Three-headed dog (6)
Voldemort's house at Hogwarts (9)
Wizard bank (9)
Wizard game (9)
Wizard gone bad (9)
____Longbottom; won points for standing up to his friends (7)

Harry Potter Sorcerer's Stone Word Search 2 Answer Key

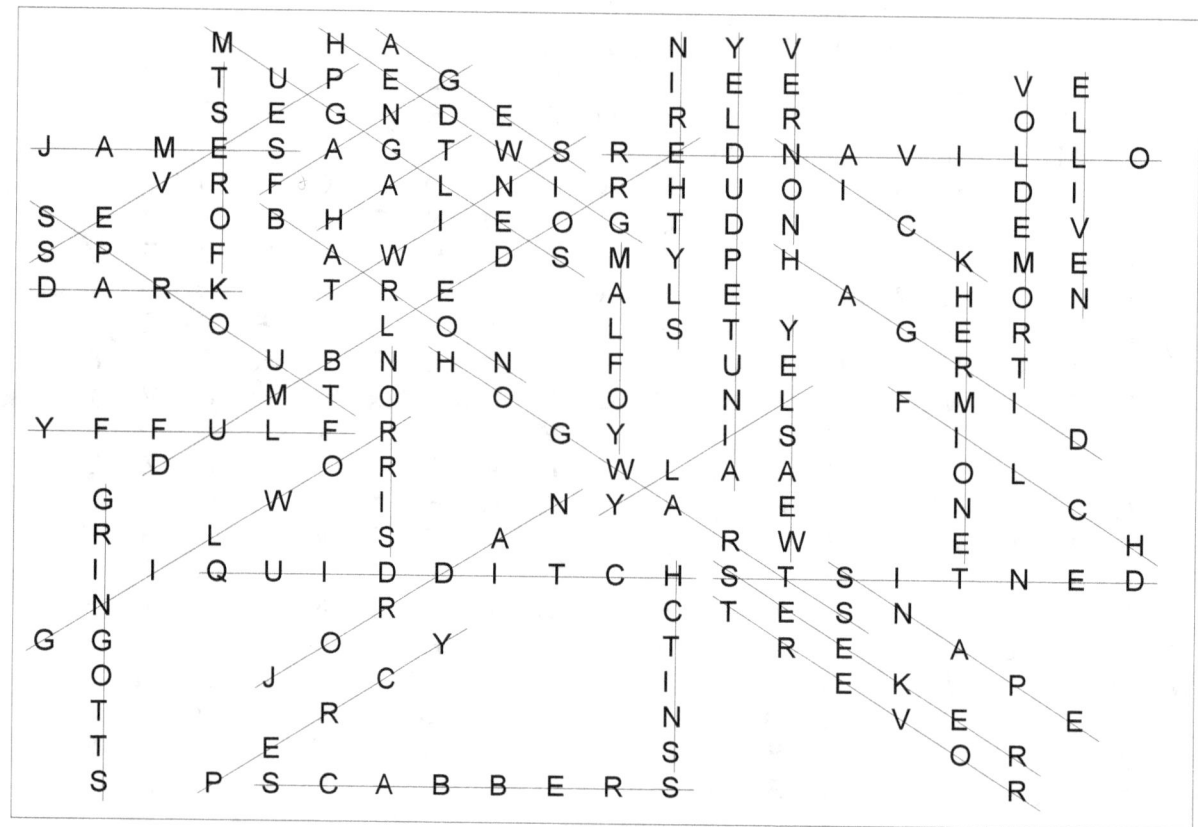

A poltergeist (6)
Author of the Harry Potter books (7)
Ball the Seeker had to catch; The Golden____ (6)
Caretaker of Hogwarts (5)
Did commentary for the Quidditch match (6)
Fred and George were ____ (5)
Girl who applies logic (8)
Hagrid's dog (4)
Harry's aunt (7)
Harry's close, red-haired friend (7)
Harry's cousin (6)
Harry's father (5)
Harry's mother (4)
Harry's owl (6)
Harry's role in Quidditch (6)
Harry's student rival (6)
Harry's uncle (6)
Headmaster of Hogwarts School (10)
Herbology professor (6)
Hermione's parents' profession (8)
Keeper of the Keys (6)
Master of Potions (5)
Mr. Filch's cat (6)

Nearly Headless____; resident ghost at Gryffindor House (4)
Neville's toad (6)
Nonmagic folk (7)
Place off-limits to students; Forbidden____ (6)
Prefect at Hogwarts;____Weasley (5)
Quidditch Through The ____; book Hermione lent Harry (4)
Quirrell's course; Defense Against the ____ Arts (4)
Ron's rat (8)
School of Witchcraft and Wizardry (8)
Seller of wands (10)
The Bloody____; Slytherin ghost (5)
The Sorting____; assigns students to houses at Hogwarts (3)
Three-headed dog (6)
Voldemort's house at Hogwarts (9)
Wizard bank (9)
Wizard game (9)
Wizard gone bad (9)
____Longbottom; won points for standing up to his friends (7)

Harry Potter Sorcerer's Stone Word Search 3

```
C V O L D E M O R T J X P G M Y R F I X
M H S H M W D Z F W H G P M X D O H N L
W R N W M N T N S Y P S Z V W J D B V Y
X H M E T N N Y V N D T D H Y Y N M I S
R H Q A R B L O Y T V S Q C M V I A S P
R E H S L Y F B R R W R K T F V F L I S
J N V L D A Y M S R V I F I D B F F B H
B O Y E Q U G Y V P I K N N X A Y O I T
L I L Y R Z D E N T I S T S G S R Y L J
D M D G Y S T L S R E F L I E O G K I F
R R R T R L M W E V M Y W L V E P W T M
Z E J B B I H Y E Y T D G E X Q K K Y W
B H F A N G N E N H E G R J M U C E J G
F M H D H W P G E H U T A O W I H L R F
W O F Z C Y B R O M P M P R N D O L P R
B A R O N C I S K T E N D D P D G I E F
B Q E E P N S N D S T I Z A E I W V T L
D B D R S X C A H X R S Z N R T A E U T
C G N Q W T A P W G T Y F N C C R N N N
Z N A X G H B E A V U V O L Y H T K I F
C I V P H G B H S T O N L F U W S N A K
B L I R A M E Y R H R G B M I F T C W D
M W L L T B R M S E P Q V C Z L F W L Q
Q O F Z Y S D V T S Y W D L N C Y P M
E R O D E L B M U D F Y L W B B V H F R
```

AGES	FOREST	JAMES	PEEVES	SNITCH
BARON	GRINGOTTS	JORDAN	PERCY	SPROUT
DARK	GRYFFINDOR	LILY	PETUNIA	TREVOR
DENTISTS	HAGRID	MALFOY	QUIDDITCH	TWINS
DUDLEY	HAT	MUGGLES	ROWLING	VERNON
DUMBLEDORE	HEDWIG	NEVILLE	SCABBERS	VOLDEMORT
FANG	HERMIONE	NICK	SEEKER	WEASLEY
FILCH	HOGWARTS	NORRIS	SLYTHERIN	
FLUFFY	INVISIBILITY	OLLIVANDER	SNAPE	

Harry Potter Sorcerer's Stone Word Search 3 Answer Key

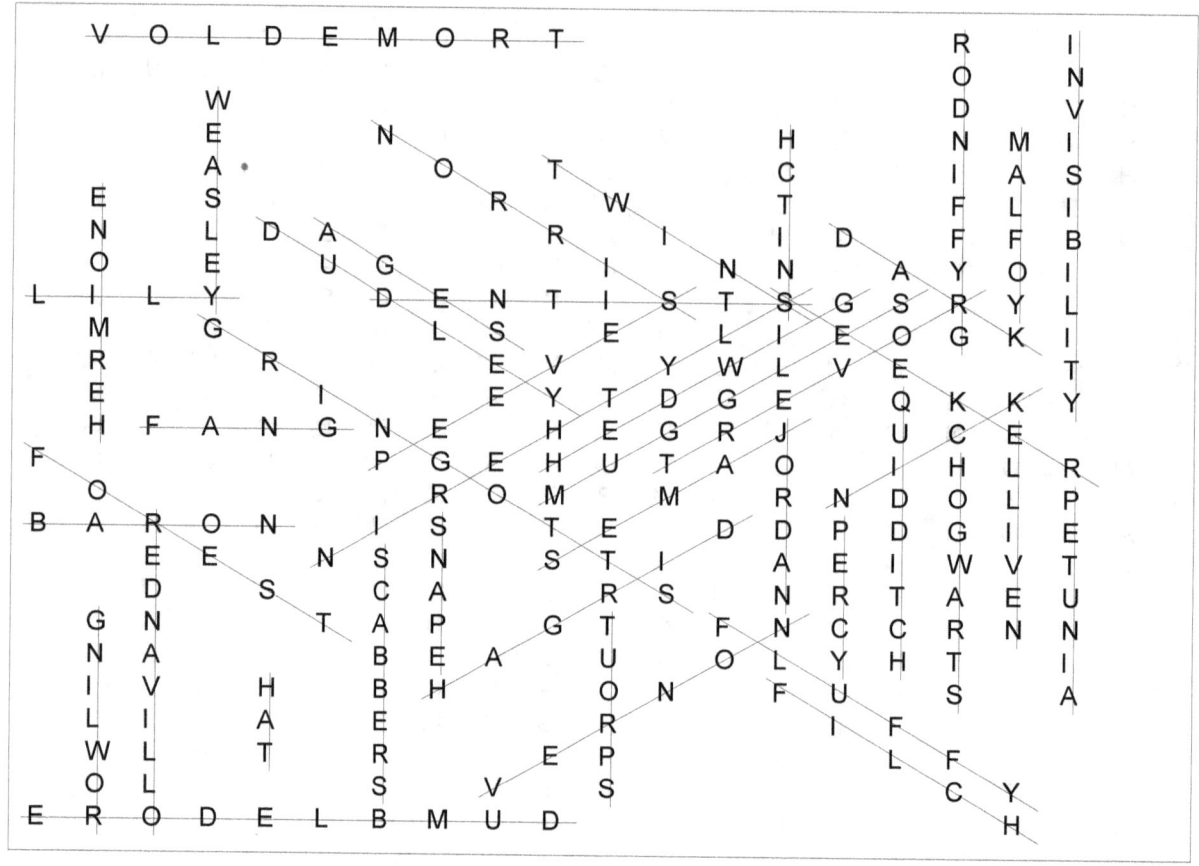

AGES	FOREST	JAMES	PEEVES	SNITCH
BARON	GRINGOTTS	JORDAN	PERCY	SPROUT
DARK	GRYFFINDOR	LILY	PETUNIA	TREVOR
DENTISTS	HAGRID	MALFOY	QUIDDITCH	TWINS
DUDLEY	HAT	MUGGLES	ROWLING	VERNON
DUMBLEDORE	HEDWIG	NEVILLE	SCABBERS	VOLDEMORT
FANG	HERMIONE	NICK	SEEKER	WEASLEY
FILCH	HOGWARTS	NORRIS	SLYTHERIN	
FLUFFY	INVISIBILITY	OLLIVANDER	SNAPE	

Harry Potter Sorcerer's Stone Word Search 4

```
N I C K X S F P E T U N I A M A L F O Y
M E L W N W E E B F V P H D U Z I P L B
Y J V I H T Q E P Y M H C D G R N D L Z
L V W I P C X V K B L N T X G Z V X I K
D T X F L M H E H E D W I G L C I S V T
F U S G L L L S J R R Z D Y E Z S W A C
Z V M G C U E Z N O J P D H S S I Z N Y
W W N B K N F M L W F C I T D L B X D W
S A C R L L H F Y L G F U G U Y I T E S
F D J S W E Y G Y I V H Q B D T L J R C
S Q P P Z Z D V M N H E W D L H I V F N
Y H T C V S J O B G X N R Y E T G N W
W T Y D D Q T F R X Z S D N Y R Y Y O Z
R N H V L H Y V J E L B M Y O I W B R K
K S O K P W N T W G R Y F F I N D O R X
R H G P G T D W A D X L Z M A G S A I N
C N W K S R W T G E V T J D S P D C S N
W H A E T Y U S E N F R R E N S E V N N
W T R E V O R C S T T O G N I R G R O F
G O T T R Y D N G I J M L O T E N R C M
F G S P Y I A H V S Y E T I C B A H J Y
W Q S D R P C H A T D D Y M H B L Y A L
C G K G E L R Z D S D L M R L A I P M R
B L A S I N H D T D P O C E Z C L F E B
K H C F W E A S L E Y V D H M S Y X S Y
```

AGES	FOREST	JAMES	PEEVES	SNITCH
BARON	GRINGOTTS	JORDAN	PERCY	SPROUT
DARK	GRYFFINDOR	LILY	PETUNIA	TREVOR
DENTISTS	HAGRID	MALFOY	QUIDDITCH	TWINS
DUDLEY	HAT	MUGGLES	ROWLING	VERNON
DUMBLEDORE	HEDWIG	NEVILLE	SCABBERS	VOLDEMORT
FANG	HERMIONE	NICK	SEEKER	WEASLEY
FILCH	HOGWARTS	NORRIS	SLYTHERIN	
FLUFFY	INVISIBILITY	OLLIVANDER	SNAPE	

Copyrighted

Harry Potter Sorcerer's Stone Word Search 4 Answer Key

AGES	FOREST	JAMES	PEEVES	SNITCH
BARON	GRINGOTTS	JORDAN	PERCY	SPROUT
DARK	GRYFFINDOR	LILY	PETUNIA	TREVOR
DENTISTS	HAGRID	MALFOY	QUIDDITCH	TWINS
DUDLEY	HAT	MUGGLES	ROWLING	VERNON
DUMBLEDORE	HEDWIG	NEVILLE	SCABBERS	VOLDEMORT
FANG	HERMIONE	NICK	SEEKER	WEASLEY
FILCH	HOGWARTS	NORRIS	SLYTHERIN	
FLUFFY	INVISIBILITY	OLLIVANDER	SNAPE	

Harry Potter Sorcerer's Stone Crossword 1

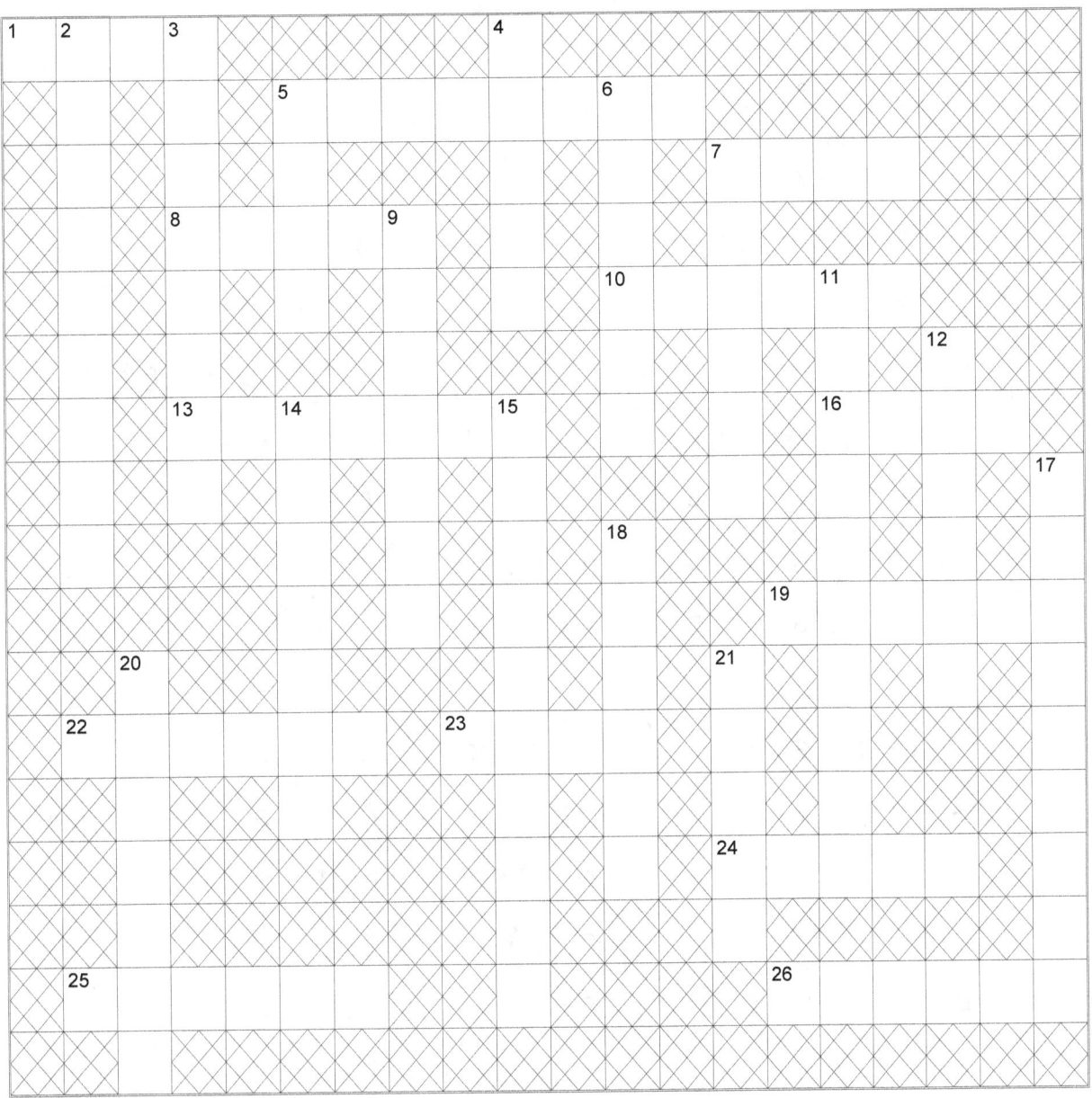

Across
1. Quidditch Through The ____; book Hermione lent Harry
5. Hermione's parents' profession
7. Hagrid's dog
8. The Bloody____; Slytherin ghost
10. Harry's uncle
13. Author of the Harry Potter books
16. Harry's mother
19. Harry's student rival
22. Harry's cousin
23. Nearly Headless____; resident ghost at Gryffindor House
24. Prefect at Hogwarts;____Weasley
25. Harry's owl
26. Did commentary for the Quidditch match

Down
2. Wizard bank
3. Ron's rat
4. Caretaker of Hogwarts
5. Quirrell's course; Defense Against the ____ Arts
6. Neville's toad
7. Place off-limits to students; Forbidden____
9. ____Longbottom; won points for standing up to his friends
11. Seller of wands
12. Three-headed dog
14. Harry's close, red-haired friend
15. Harry's house at Hogwarts
17. Voldemort's house at Hogwarts
18. Harry's role in Quidditch
20. Nonmagic folk
21. Master of Potions

Harry Potter Sorcerer's Stone Crossword 1 Answer Key

	1 A	2 G	3 E	S			4 F					
		R		C	5 D	E	N	T	I	6 S	T	S
		I		A	A			L		R	7 F	A	N	G
		N	8 B	A	R	O	9 N		C	E	O	
		G	B		K		E		H	10 V	E	R	N	O	11 N
		O	E				V			O	E		L	12 F
		T	13 R	14 W	L	I	15 N	G		R	S		16 L	I	L	Y
		T	S	E			L	R			T	I		U	17 S
		S		A			L	Y		18 S			V	F	L
				S		E		F		E		19 M	A	L	F	O	Y
		20 M		L			F		21 S	N		Y	T
		22 D	U	D	L	E	Y	23 N	I	C	K	N	D		H
		G		Y			N	E	A	E		E
		G					D	R	24 P	E	R	C	Y	R
		L					O		E			I
	25 H	E	D	W	I	G	R			26 J	O	R	D	A	N
		S										

Across
1. Quidditch Through The ____; book Hermione lent Harry
5. Hermione's parents' profession
7. Hagrid's dog
8. The Bloody____; Slytherin ghost
10. Harry's uncle
13. Author of the Harry Potter books
16. Harry's mother
19. Harry's student rival
22. Harry's cousin
23. Nearly Headless____; resident ghost at Gryffindor House
24. Prefect at Hogwarts;____Weasley
25. Harry's owl
26. Did commentary for the Quidditch match

Down
2. Wizard bank
3. Ron's rat
4. Caretaker of Hogwarts
5. Quirrell's course; Defense Against the ____ Arts
6. Neville's toad
7. Place off-limits to students; Forbidden____
9. ____Longbottom; won points for standing up to his friends
11. Seller of wands
12. Three-headed dog
14. Harry's close, red-haired friend
15. Harry's house at Hogwarts
17. Voldemort's house at Hogwarts
18. Harry's role in Quidditch
20. Nonmagic folk
21. Master of Potions

Harry Potter Sorcerer's Stone Crossword 2

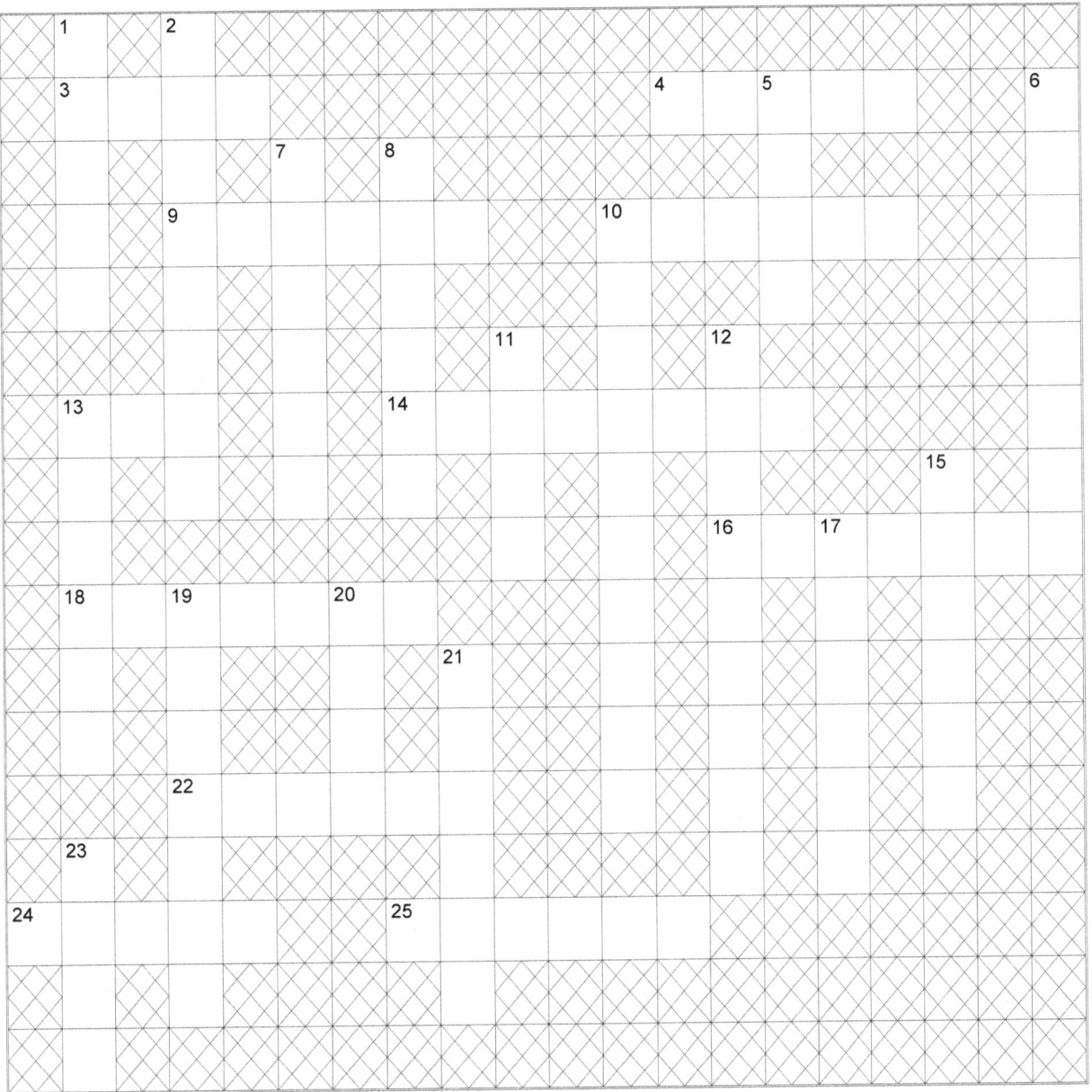

Across
- 3. Quidditch Through The ____; book Hermione lent Harry
- 4. Caretaker of Hogwarts
- 9. Neville's toad
- 10. Harry's cousin
- 13. The Sorting____; assigns students to houses at Hogwarts
- 14. Ron's rat
- 16. ____Longbottom; won points for standing up to his friends
- 18. Author of the Harry Potter books
- 22. Harry's role in Quidditch
- 24. Harry's father
- 25. Harry's student rival

Down
- 1. The Bloody____; Slytherin ghost
- 2. Hermione's parents' profession
- 5. Harry's mother
- 6. Girl who applies logic
- 7. Harry's owl
- 8. Place off-limits to students; Forbidden____
- 10. Headmaster of Hogwarts School
- 11. Quirrell's course; Defense Against the ____ Arts
- 12. Wizard bank
- 13. Keeper of the Keys
- 15. Three-headed dog
- 17. Harry's uncle
- 19. Harry's close, red-haired friend
- 20. Nearly Headless____; resident ghost at Gryffindor House
- 21. Did commentary for the Quidditch match
- 23. Hagrid's dog

Harry Potter Sorcerer's Stone Crossword 2 Answer Key

	1 B	2 D										
3	A	G	E	S			4 F	5 I	L	C	H	6 H
	R	N	7 H	8 F				I				E
	O	9 T	R	E	V	O	R	10 D	U	D	L	E	Y	R
	N	I		D	R			U		Y		M
		S		W	E	11 D		12 M	G			I
13 H	A	T		I	14 S	C	A	B	B	E	R	S	O
	A	S		G	T	R		L		I		15 F	N
	G				K	E		16 N	17 E	V	I	L	L	E
18 R	O	19 W	L	20 I	N	G		D	G		E		U
	I	E		I	21 J		O	O		R	F
	D	A		C	O		R	T		N	F
		22 S	E	E	K	E	R	E		T	O	Y
23 F	L			R	D		S	N
24 J	A	M	E	S	25 M	A	L	F	O	Y
	N	Y		N
	G

Across
- 3. Quidditch Through The ____; book Hermione lent Harry
- 4. Caretaker of Hogwarts
- 9. Neville's toad
- 10. Harry's cousin
- 13. The Sorting____; assigns students to houses at Hogwarts
- 14. Ron's rat
- 16. ____Longbottom; won points for standing up to his friends
- 18. Author of the Harry Potter books
- 22. Harry's role in Quidditch
- 24. Harry's father
- 25. Harry's student rival

Down
- 1. The Bloody____; Slytherin ghost
- 2. Hermione's parents' profession
- 5. Harry's mother
- 6. Girl who applies logic
- 7. Harry's owl
- 8. Place off-limits to students; Forbidden____
- 10. Headmaster of Hogwarts School
- 11. Quirrell's course; Defense Against the ____ Arts
- 12. Wizard bank
- 13. Keeper of the Keys
- 15. Three-headed dog
- 17. Harry's uncle
- 19. Harry's close, red-haired friend
- 20. Nearly Headless____; resident ghost at Gryffindor House
- 21. Did commentary for the Quidditch match
- 23. Hagrid's dog

Harry Potter Sorcerer's Stone Crossword 3

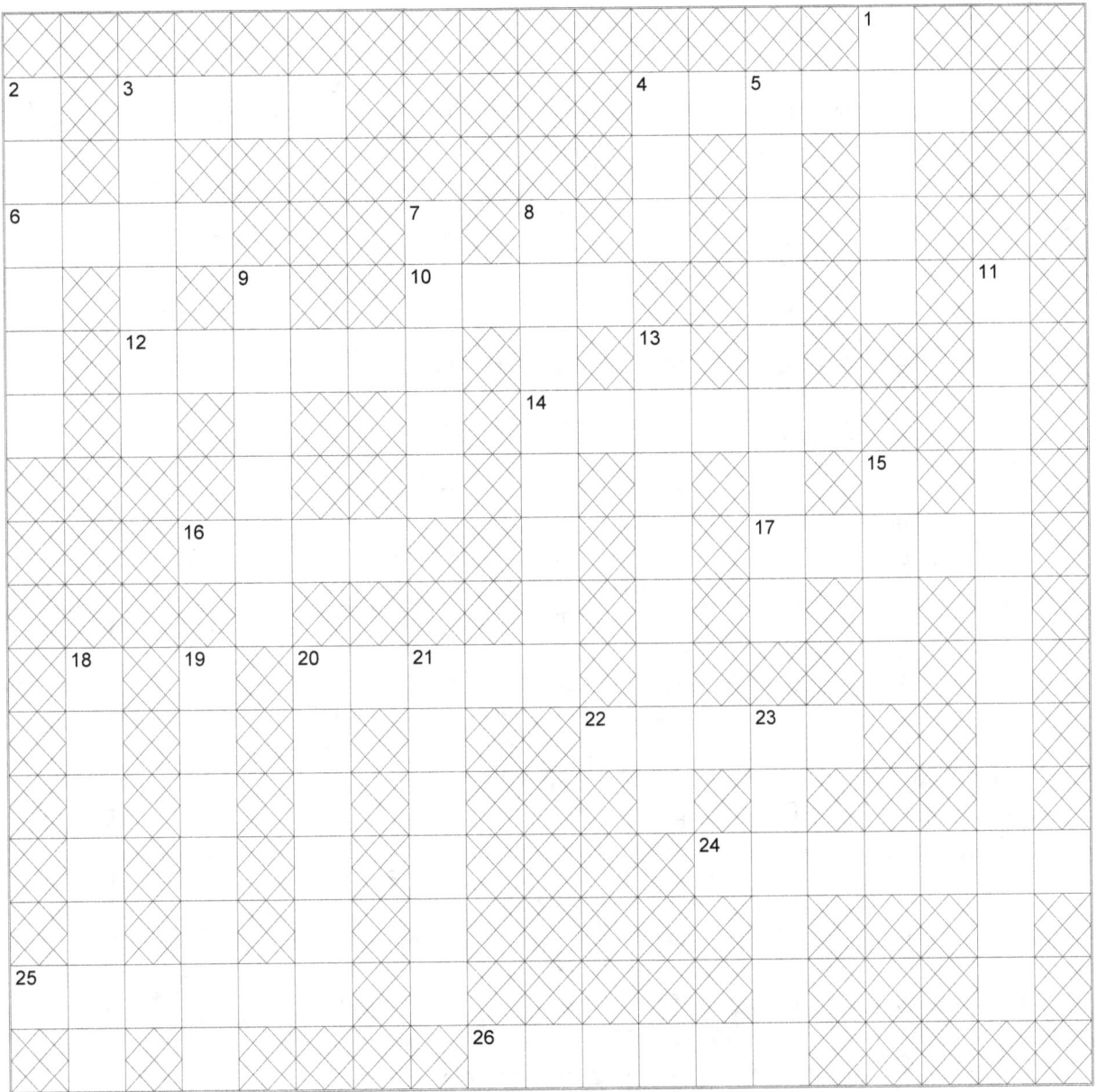

Across
- 3. Hagrid's dog
- 4. Keeper of the Keys
- 6. Quirrell's course; Defense Against the ____ Arts
- 10. Quidditch Through The ____; book Hermione lent Harry
- 12. Harry's role in Quidditch
- 14. Neville's toad
- 16. Harry's mother
- 17. Fred and George were ____
- 20. Harry's father
- 22. Master of Potions
- 24. Harry's aunt
- 25. Harry's uncle
- 26. Mr. Filch's cat

Down
- 1. Caretaker of Hogwarts
- 2. Harry's cousin
- 3. Place off-limits to students; Forbidden____
- 4. The Sorting____; assigns students to houses at Hogwarts
- 5. Wizard bank
- 7. The Bloody____; Slytherin ghost
- 8. Hermione's parents' profession
- 9. Harry's owl
- 11. "Just in case" note was left on the ____Cloak
- 13. Girl who applies logic
- 15. Nearly Headless____; resident ghost at Gryffindor House
- 18. Nonmagic folk
- 19. Author of the Harry Potter books
- 20. Did commentary for the Quidditch match
- 21. Harry's student rival
- 23. A poltergeist

Harry Potter Sorcerer's Stone Crossword 3 Answer Key

		2 D		3 F	A	N	G			4 H	5 G	A	1 F R	I	D
		U		O						A	R		L		
		6 D	A	R	K		7 B		8 D	T	I		C		
		L		E		9 H	A	10 G	E	S	N		H		11 I
		E		12 S	E	E	K	E	R	13 H	G				N
		Y		T		D		O	14 T	R	E	V	O	R	V
						W		N	I	R	T		15 N		I
				16 L	I	L	Y		S	M		17 T	W	I	N	S
				G					T	I		S		C		I
		18 M	19 R	20 J	A	21 M	E	S		O			K		B
		U	O	O		A			22 S	N	A	23 P	E		I
		G	W	R		L			E			E			L
		G	L	D		F			24 P	E	T	U	N	I	A
		L	I	A		O						V			T
25 V	E	R	N	O	N							E			Y
		S	G			26 N	O	R	R	I	S				

Across
- 3. Hagrid's dog
- 4. Keeper of the Keys
- 6. Quirrell's course; Defense Against the ____ Arts
- 10. Quidditch Through The ____; book Hermione lent Harry
- 12. Harry's role in Quidditch
- 14. Neville's toad
- 16. Harry's mother
- 17. Fred and George were ____
- 20. Harry's father
- 22. Master of Potions
- 24. Harry's aunt
- 25. Harry's uncle
- 26. Mr. Filch's cat

Down
- 1. Caretaker of Hogwarts
- 2. Harry's cousin
- 3. Place off-limits to students; Forbidden____
- 4. The Sorting____; assigns students to houses at Hogwarts
- 5. Wizard bank
- 7. The Bloody____; Slytherin ghost
- 8. Hermione's parents' profession
- 9. Harry's owl
- 11. "Just in case" note was left on the ____Cloak
- 13. Girl who applies logic
- 15. Nearly Headless____; resident ghost at Gryffindor House
- 18. Nonmagic folk
- 19. Author of the Harry Potter books
- 20. Did commentary for the Quidditch match
- 21. Harry's student rival
- 23. A poltergeist

Harry Potter Sorcerer's Stone Crossword 4

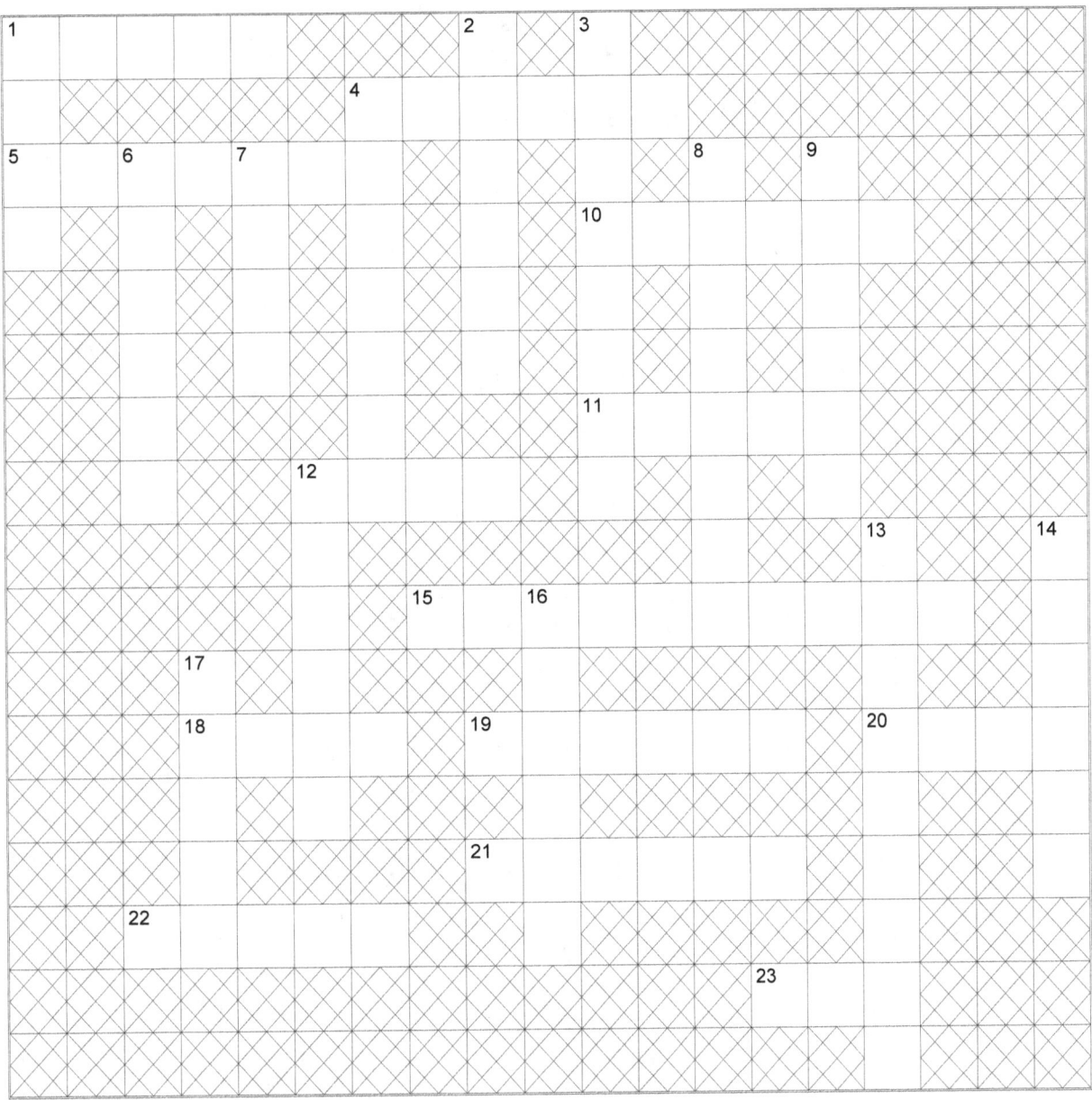

Across
1. Caretaker of Hogwarts
4. A poltergeist
5. ____Longbottom; won points for standing up to his friends
10. Neville's toad
11. Fred and George were ____
12. Quirrell's course; Defense Against the ____ Arts
15. Headmaster of Hogwarts School
18. Quidditch Through The ____; book Hermione lent Harry
19. Three-headed dog
20. Nearly Headless____; resident ghost at Gryffindor House
21. Did commentary for the Quidditch match
22. Master of Potions
23. The Sorting____; assigns students to houses at Hogwarts

Down
1. Hagrid's dog
2. Harry's owl
3. Hermione's parents' profession
4. Harry's aunt
6. Harry's uncle
7. Harry's mother
8. Girl who applies logic
9. Place off-limits to students; Forbidden____
12. Harry's cousin
13. Wizard bank
14. Harry's role in Quidditch
16. Harry's student rival
17. The Bloody____; Slytherin ghost

Harry Potter Sorcerer's Stone Crossword 4 Answer Key

Across
1. Caretaker of Hogwarts
4. A poltergeist
5. ____Longbottom; won points for standing up to his friends
10. Neville's toad
11. Fred and George were ____
12. Quirrell's course; Defense Against the ____ Arts
15. Headmaster of Hogwarts School
18. Quidditch Through The ____; book Hermione lent Harry
19. Three-headed dog
20. Nearly Headless____; resident ghost at Gryffindor House
21. Did commentary for the Quidditch match
22. Master of Potions
23. The Sorting____; assigns students to houses at Hogwarts

Down
1. Hagrid's dog
2. Harry's owl
3. Hermione's parents' profession
4. Harry's aunt
6. Harry's uncle
7. Harry's mother
8. Girl who applies logic
9. Place off-limits to students; Forbidden____
12. Harry's cousin
13. Wizard bank
14. Harry's role in Quidditch
16. Harry's student rival
17. The Bloody____; Slytherin ghost

Harry Potter Sorcerer's Stone

JORDAN	AGES	NORRIS	VOLDEMORT	NEVILLE
MALFOY	SCABBERS	LILY	JAMES	TREVOR
DENTISTS	FLUFFY	FREE SPACE	QUIDDITCH	INVISIBILITY
PETUNIA	FANG	PERCY	GRINGOTTS	ROWLING
SLYTHERIN	SPROUT	TWINS	HAT	VERNON

Harry Potter Sorcerer's Stone

SNAPE	GRYFFINDOR	FOREST	DARK	MUGGLES
PEEVES	OLLIVANDER	HEDWIG	HERMIONE	HOGWARTS
SEEKER	HAGRID	FREE SPACE	SNITCH	DUDLEY
BARON	WEASLEY	DUMBLEDORE	VERNON	HAT
TWINS	SPROUT	SLYTHERIN	ROWLING	GRINGOTTS

Harry Potter Sorcerer's Stone

ROWLING	DUDLEY	SNAPE	JAMES	JORDAN
VERNON	SNITCH	FOREST	HEDWIG	NICK
DENTISTS	INVISIBILITY	FREE SPACE	NEVILLE	AGES
HAGRID	QUIDDITCH	HOGWARTS	SEEKER	TREVOR
GRINGOTTS	FILCH	MALFOY	FLUFFY	OLLIVANDER

Harry Potter Sorcerer's Stone

DARK	PETUNIA	SLYTHERIN	HAT	PERCY
PEEVES	FANG	MUGGLES	GRYFFINDOR	TWINS
SPROUT	VOLDEMORT	FREE SPACE	LILY	BARON
DUMBLEDORE	NORRIS	WEASLEY	OLLIVANDER	FLUFFY
MALFOY	FILCH	GRINGOTTS	TREVOR	SEEKER

Harry Potter Sorcerer's Stone

SNAPE	HEDWIG	OLLIVANDER	NEVILLE	SEEKER
AGES	FANG	ROWLING	SPROUT	SLYTHERIN
TWINS	NORRIS	FREE SPACE	PEEVES	DUDLEY
DUMBLEDORE	SCABBERS	FLUFFY	GRINGOTTS	JAMES
HAGRID	HERMIONE	TREVOR	PETUNIA	QUIDDITCH

Harry Potter Sorcerer's Stone

NICK	LILY	JORDAN	GRYFFINDOR	FILCH
PERCY	INVISIBILITY	BARON	VOLDEMORT	HOGWARTS
FOREST	MUGGLES	FREE SPACE	VERNON	HAT
DENTISTS	WEASLEY	SNITCH	QUIDDITCH	PETUNIA
TREVOR	HERMIONE	HAGRID	JAMES	GRINGOTTS

Harry Potter Sorcerer's Stone

MALFOY	GRINGOTTS	QUIDDITCH	OLLIVANDER	JORDAN
HERMIONE	HAT	SNITCH	BARON	JAMES
DUDLEY	DARK	FREE SPACE	VOLDEMORT	LILY
ROWLING	SNAPE	FOREST	WEASLEY	PERCY
SPROUT	PEEVES	PETUNIA	HAGRID	INVISIBILITY

Harry Potter Sorcerer's Stone

SEEKER	DUMBLEDORE	FILCH	FANG	NORRIS
HEDWIG	SLYTHERIN	AGES	NEVILLE	NICK
TWINS	HOGWARTS	FREE SPACE	VERNON	DENTISTS
GRYFFINDOR	FLUFFY	TREVOR	INVISIBILITY	HAGRID
PETUNIA	PEEVES	SPROUT	PERCY	WEASLEY

Harry Potter Sorcerer's Stone

JORDAN	AGES	FILCH	SPROUT	TWINS
JAMES	SNAPE	HAT	ROWLING	NEVILLE
WEASLEY	QUIDDITCH	FREE SPACE	LILY	NICK
HAGRID	PERCY	BARON	INVISIBILITY	FANG
FOREST	DUDLEY	MUGGLES	HOGWARTS	PETUNIA

Harry Potter Sorcerer's Stone

DUMBLEDORE	GRINGOTTS	HEDWIG	OLLIVANDER	TREVOR
VERNON	DARK	NORRIS	DENTISTS	SEEKER
SLYTHERIN	MALFOY	FREE SPACE	VOLDEMORT	FLUFFY
PEEVES	SNITCH	SCABBERS	PETUNIA	HOGWARTS
MUGGLES	DUDLEY	FOREST	FANG	INVISIBILITY

Harry Potter Sorcerer's Stone

FOREST	SEEKER	HAGRID	ROWLING	JORDAN
LILY	AGES	FILCH	MUGGLES	DUDLEY
JAMES	HAT	FREE SPACE	PERCY	FLUFFY
DARK	SCABBERS	WEASLEY	HOGWARTS	HEDWIG
TREVOR	VERNON	BARON	SNAPE	FANG

Harry Potter Sorcerer's Stone

NICK	VOLDEMORT	DENTISTS	GRINGOTTS	OLLIVANDER
DUMBLEDORE	GRYFFINDOR	SPROUT	MALFOY	TWINS
QUIDDITCH	HERMIONE	FREE SPACE	SNITCH	NEVILLE
NORRIS	PEEVES	PETUNIA	FANG	SNAPE
BARON	VERNON	TREVOR	HEDWIG	HOGWARTS

Harry Potter Sorcerer's Stone

DARK	TREVOR	LILY	MUGGLES	NICK
HAGRID	GRYFFINDOR	AGES	SNAPE	JORDAN
NEVILLE	OLLIVANDER	FREE SPACE	SCABBERS	FILCH
PEEVES	INVISIBILITY	VOLDEMORT	PETUNIA	DUDLEY
TWINS	DENTISTS	HERMIONE	PERCY	BARON

Harry Potter Sorcerer's Stone

FLUFFY	SLYTHERIN	ROWLING	WEASLEY	GRINGOTTS
FANG	FOREST	SPROUT	HOGWARTS	SNITCH
NORRIS	JAMES	FREE SPACE	VERNON	HEDWIG
QUIDDITCH	DUMBLEDORE	MALFOY	BARON	PERCY
HERMIONE	DENTISTS	TWINS	DUDLEY	PETUNIA

Harry Potter Sorcerer's Stone

MUGGLES	VERNON	MALFOY	SNITCH	HAT
DENTISTS	DUDLEY	SLYTHERIN	LILY	SPROUT
DUMBLEDORE	BARON	FREE SPACE	INVISIBILITY	VOLDEMORT
HAGRID	WEASLEY	PERCY	FILCH	DARK
SEEKER	HEDWIG	NORRIS	TWINS	PETUNIA

Harry Potter Sorcerer's Stone

PEEVES	SCABBERS	OLLIVANDER	NICK	FANG
FLUFFY	GRYFFINDOR	AGES	JAMES	TREVOR
GRINGOTTS	JORDAN	FREE SPACE	NEVILLE	HOGWARTS
QUIDDITCH	HERMIONE	FOREST	PETUNIA	TWINS
NORRIS	HEDWIG	SEEKER	DARK	FILCH

Harry Potter Sorcerer's Stone

FLUFFY	GRYFFINDOR	MUGGLES	HERMIONE	FANG
JORDAN	VERNON	LILY	SLYTHERIN	PERCY
INVISIBILITY	QUIDDITCH	FREE SPACE	HAT	GRINGOTTS
OLLIVANDER	NEVILLE	PEEVES	WEASLEY	SNAPE
NICK	SEEKER	VOLDEMORT	NORRIS	DENTISTS

Harry Potter Sorcerer's Stone

HAGRID	MALFOY	JAMES	BARON	DARK
SCABBERS	DUMBLEDORE	TREVOR	SNITCH	TWINS
DUDLEY	PETUNIA	FREE SPACE	SPROUT	AGES
ROWLING	FILCH	HOGWARTS	DENTISTS	NORRIS
VOLDEMORT	SEEKER	NICK	SNAPE	WEASLEY

Harry Potter Sorcerer's Stone

PETUNIA	JAMES	FOREST	HERMIONE	FILCH
ROWLING	SNAPE	WEASLEY	JORDAN	GRINGOTTS
NORRIS	NICK	FREE SPACE	VOLDEMORT	HOGWARTS
MALFOY	HAT	DENTISTS	OLLIVANDER	SNITCH
FLUFFY	TWINS	HEDWIG	BARON	SLYTHERIN

Harry Potter Sorcerer's Stone

VERNON	AGES	DARK	FANG	QUIDDITCH
LILY	SCABBERS	SPROUT	NEVILLE	DUDLEY
PERCY	INVISIBILITY	FREE SPACE	PEEVES	SEEKER
DUMBLEDORE	MUGGLES	HAGRID	SLYTHERIN	BARON
HEDWIG	TWINS	FLUFFY	SNITCH	OLLIVANDER

Harry Potter Sorcerer's Stone

DENTISTS	HEDWIG	PERCY	FOREST	LILY
FILCH	ROWLING	AGES	BARON	PETUNIA
OLLIVANDER	NICK	FREE SPACE	SNITCH	DUMBLEDORE
JORDAN	JAMES	SCABBERS	NORRIS	HERMIONE
DARK	GRINGOTTS	GRYFFINDOR	VOLDEMORT	INVISIBILITY

Harry Potter Sorcerer's Stone

SEEKER	DUDLEY	PEEVES	HAT	QUIDDITCH
HAGRID	FANG	HOGWARTS	TREVOR	NEVILLE
SPROUT	TWINS	FREE SPACE	WEASLEY	VERNON
FLUFFY	MALFOY	MUGGLES	INVISIBILITY	VOLDEMORT
GRYFFINDOR	GRINGOTTS	DARK	HERMIONE	NORRIS

Harry Potter Sorcerer's Stone

PERCY	DENTISTS	SPROUT	WEASLEY	PEEVES
SNAPE	HAT	OLLIVANDER	INVISIBILITY	FANG
DUDLEY	HOGWARTS	FREE SPACE	LILY	FLUFFY
FILCH	MUGGLES	HAGRID	DUMBLEDORE	TREVOR
VOLDEMORT	TWINS	VERNON	JORDAN	JAMES

Harry Potter Sorcerer's Stone

HERMIONE	GRINGOTTS	DARK	MALFOY	NEVILLE
AGES	SEEKER	SNITCH	SLYTHERIN	NICK
NORRIS	SCABBERS	FREE SPACE	GRYFFINDOR	HEDWIG
BARON	ROWLING	QUIDDITCH	JAMES	JORDAN
VERNON	TWINS	VOLDEMORT	TREVOR	DUMBLEDORE

Harry Potter Sorcerer's Stone

PEEVES	DENTISTS	GRINGOTTS	BARON	HEDWIG
JAMES	NORRIS	MALFOY	SNAPE	DUDLEY
NEVILLE	DARK	FREE SPACE	GRYFFINDOR	VOLDEMORT
FLUFFY	SPROUT	MUGGLES	LILY	HOGWARTS
NICK	SLYTHERIN	DUMBLEDORE	TREVOR	AGES

Harry Potter Sorcerer's Stone

FOREST	SEEKER	PETUNIA	HERMIONE	JORDAN
SCABBERS	OLLIVANDER	VERNON	ROWLING	FANG
TWINS	SNITCH	FREE SPACE	INVISIBILITY	HAGRID
PERCY	WEASLEY	QUIDDITCH	AGES	TREVOR
DUMBLEDORE	SLYTHERIN	NICK	HOGWARTS	LILY

Harry Potter Sorcerer's Stone

BARON	TWINS	SNITCH	NORRIS	INVISIBILITY
JORDAN	AGES	NICK	DUMBLEDORE	ROWLING
MALFOY	WEASLEY	FREE SPACE	FOREST	HERMIONE
FILCH	HAGRID	NEVILLE	VOLDEMORT	SNAPE
SCABBERS	FANG	VERNON	TREVOR	DARK

Harry Potter Sorcerer's Stone

HOGWARTS	FLUFFY	SEEKER	SLYTHERIN	GRINGOTTS
HEDWIG	PETUNIA	LILY	HAT	DENTISTS
PERCY	OLLIVANDER	FREE SPACE	QUIDDITCH	SPROUT
GRYFFINDOR	DUDLEY	PEEVES	DARK	TREVOR
VERNON	FANG	SCABBERS	SNAPE	VOLDEMORT

Harry Potter Sorcerer's Stone

SPROUT	SNAPE	MALFOY	HAT	HERMIONE
GRINGOTTS	JAMES	AGES	VOLDEMORT	MUGGLES
OLLIVANDER	QUIDDITCH	FREE SPACE	TWINS	PEEVES
DARK	SLYTHERIN	HOGWARTS	SEEKER	NEVILLE
VERNON	PERCY	FLUFFY	TREVOR	FILCH

Harry Potter Sorcerer's Stone

FANG	HAGRID	ROWLING	DUMBLEDORE	HEDWIG
NICK	NORRIS	LILY	WEASLEY	SCABBERS
GRYFFINDOR	INVISIBILITY	FREE SPACE	BARON	PETUNIA
FOREST	JORDAN	SNITCH	FILCH	TREVOR
FLUFFY	PERCY	VERNON	NEVILLE	SEEKER

Harry Potter Sorcerer's Stone

PERCY	DENTISTS	ROWLING	MUGGLES	DUMBLEDORE
SNITCH	JAMES	SEEKER	PETUNIA	WEASLEY
FILCH	GRINGOTTS	FREE SPACE	PEEVES	NEVILLE
HAGRID	SLYTHERIN	AGES	HAT	GRYFFINDOR
LILY	FOREST	DUDLEY	SPROUT	INVISIBILITY

Harry Potter Sorcerer's Stone

SCABBERS	HOGWARTS	BARON	TREVOR	JORDAN
HEDWIG	SNAPE	OLLIVANDER	FLUFFY	VERNON
HERMIONE	VOLDEMORT	FREE SPACE	MALFOY	TWINS
DARK	QUIDDITCH	FANG	INVISIBILITY	SPROUT
DUDLEY	FOREST	LILY	GRYFFINDOR	HAT

Sorcerer's Stone Vocabulary Word List

No.	Word	Clue/Definition
1.	AGONY	Extreme pain
2.	AJAR	Partially open
3.	AMAZEMENT	Wonder
4.	BABBLE	Foolish talk
5.	BIASED	Prejudiced
6.	BLURTED	Said impulsively
7.	BURLY	Husky
8.	CAULDRON	Large kettle for boiling
9.	CLAMBERED	Climbed with difficulty
10.	CLOAKS	Loose outer garments
11.	CLOBBERED	Battered
12.	CONVINCED	Certain
13.	COWERING	Cringing
14.	CRANING	Stretching, straining
15.	CRINKLED	Wrinkled
16.	DANGLING	Hanging loosely
17.	DESPERATE	Nearly hopeless
18.	DESTINY	Fate
19.	DUNDERHEAD	Dunce, dummy
20.	ELIXIR	Special medicine
21.	ENORMOUS	Very big
22.	ERUPTED	Burst, spewed
23.	EXPELLED	Forced, put out
24.	FASCINATED	Intensely interested
25.	FEEBLE	Weak
26.	FLINCHED	Winced
27.	FLING	Throw
28.	FORBIDDEN	Not allowed
29.	FURIOUSLY	Angrily
30.	FURY	Intense anger, rage
31.	GALOSHES	Waterproof overshoes
32.	GLEE	Joy
33.	GLISTENING	Glittering
34.	GLOATINGLY	In a self-satisfied way
35.	GLOOMY	Dark, dreary
36.	GOBLIN	Grotesque elfin creature
37.	GOGGLE	Stare
38.	GRAPPLING	Struggling
39.	GRUDGINGLY	Reluctantly
40.	GRUFFLY	Harshly
41.	HAGS	Witches
42.	HORRIFIED	Very shocked
43.	HOVERING	Floating suspended in air
44.	INSTINCT	Natural behavior
45.	INTERFERING	Meddling, bothering, in the way
46.	JOSTLED	Pushed, elbowed
47.	KNACK	Special talent
48.	KNICKERBOCKERS	Full pants gathered below the knee
49.	LADEN	Burdened
50.	LINGERED	Delayed leaving
51.	MANGLED	Torn, mutilated
52.	MIFFED	Annoyed
53.	MUMBLING	Speaking unclearly

Sorcerer's Stone Vocabulary Word List

No.	Word	Clue/Definition
54.	MUTELY	Silently
55.	MYSTIFIED	Bewildered, perplexed
56.	OMEN	Sign
57.	PECULIAR	Odd, unusual
58.	PELTING	Hurling
59.	PETRIFIED	Paralyzed with terror
60.	PLUMP	Chubby, full in figure
61.	POLTERGEIST	Ghost that announces its presence
62.	PREFECT	Student officer
63.	PUB	Tavern, bar
64.	QUAILED	Shrank in fear
65.	REFLECTION	Image as from a mirror
66.	REMORSE	Regret
67.	RUBBISH	Garbage, trash
68.	RUFFLED	Disturbed, annoyed
69.	SACKED	Fired, let go
70.	SAVAGING	Attacking violently
71.	SCOWL	Angry frown
72.	SCRABBLING	Scraping
73.	SEIZED	Grabbed
74.	SHUDDERED	Shivered, as from fear or aversion
75.	SHUFFLED	Walked while dragging feet
76.	SLITHER	Slide, glide
77.	SNARLED	Growled
78.	SNEER	Scornful facial expression
79.	SNIGGERED	Snickered
80.	SPECTACLES	Glasses
81.	STERN	Firm, severe
82.	SUPPOSED	Assumed to be true
83.	TANTRUM	Fit
84.	TENDRILS	Stems, shoots
85.	TIDY	Neat
86.	TIMIDLY	Hesitantly
87.	THRASHING	Beating, flailing
88.	TRODDEN	Walked on
89.	TUFTS	Short strands of hair
90.	URGENT	Needing immediate action
91.	WAFTING	Moving gently
92.	WHACKED	Struck, hit
93.	WHEELED	Turned suddenly
94.	WHITTLED	Cut, carved
95.	WIZARD	Magician

Sorcerer's Stone Vocabulary Fill In The Blank 1

_____ 1. Image as from a mirror

_____ 2. Assumed to be true

_____ 3. Foolish talk

_____ 4. Shivered, as from fear or aversion

_____ 5. Disturbed, annoyed

_____ 6. Full pants gathered below the knee

_____ 7. Battered

_____ 8. Said impulsively

_____ 9. Struck, hit

_____ 10. Tavern, bar

_____ 11. Walked while dragging feet

_____ 12. Magician

_____ 13. Delay

_____ 14. Firm, severe

_____ 15. Natural behavior

_____ 16. Neat

_____ 17. Extreme pain

_____ 18. Fired, let go

_____ 19. Meddling, bothering, in the way

_____ 20. Pushed, elbowed

Sorcerer's Stone Vocabulary Fill In The Blank 1 Answer Key

REFLECTION	1. Image as from a mirror
SUPPOSED	2. Assumed to be true
BABBLE	3. Foolish talk
SHUDDERED	4. Shivered, as from fear or aversion
RUFFLED	5. Disturbed, annoyed
KNICKERBOCKERS	6. Full pants gathered below the knee
CLOBBERED	7. Battered
BLURTED	8. Said impulsively
WHACKED	9. Struck, hit
PUB	10. Tavern, bar
SHUFFLED	11. Walked while dragging feet
WIZARD	12. Magician
HITCH	13. Delay
STERN	14. Firm, severe
INSTINCT	15. Natural behavior
TIDY	16. Neat
AGONY	17. Extreme pain
SACKED	18. Fired, let go
INTERFERING	19. Meddling, bothering, in the way
JOSTLED	20. Pushed, elbowed

Sorcerer's Stone Vocabulary Fill In The Blank 2

_____ 1. Floating suspended in air

_____ 2. Fate

_____ 3. Weak

_____ 4. Intensely interested

_____ 5. Odd, unusual

_____ 6. Nearly hopeless

_____ 7. Very shocked

_____ 8. Loose outer garments

_____ 9. Struggling

_____ 10. Regret

_____ 11. Stretching, straining

_____ 12. Snickered

_____ 13. Stare

_____ 14. Student officer

_____ 15. Extreme pain

_____ 16. Burst, spewed

_____ 17. Special medicine

_____ 18. Disturbed, annoyed

_____ 19. Wonder

_____ 20. Short strands of hair

Sorcerer's Stone Vocabulary Fill In The Blank 2 Answer Key

HOVERING	1. Floating suspended in air
DESTINY	2. Fate
FEEBLE	3. Weak
FASCINATED	4. Intensely interested
PECULIAR	5. Odd, unusual
DESPERATE	6. Nearly hopeless
HORRIFIED	7. Very shocked
CLOAKS	8. Loose outer garments
GRAPPLING	9. Struggling
REMORSE	10. Regret
CRANING	11. Stretching, straining
SNIGGERED	12. Snickered
GOGGLE	13. Stare
PREFECT	14. Student officer
AGONY	15. Extreme pain
ERUPTED	16. Burst, spewed
ELIXIR	17. Special medicine
RUFFLED	18. Disturbed, annoyed
AMAZEMENT	19. Wonder
TUFTS	20. Short strands of hair

Sorcerer's Stone Vocabulary Fill In The Blank 3

_____ 1. Paralyzed with terror

_____ 2. Annoyed

_____ 3. Image as from a mirror

_____ 4. Struck, hit

_____ 5. Harshly

_____ 6. Needing immediate action

_____ 7. Husky

_____ 8. Hesitantly

_____ 9. Burdened

_____ 10. Bewildered, perplexed

_____ 11. Prejudiced

_____ 12. Nearly hopeless

_____ 13. Battered

_____ 14. Odd, unusual

_____ 15. Hurling

_____ 16. Said impulsively

_____ 17. Fit

_____ 18. Fate

_____ 19. Cringing

_____ 20. Climbed with difficulty

Sorcerer's Stone Vocabulary Fill In The Blank 3 Answer Key

PETRIFIED	1. Paralyzed with terror
MIFFED	2. Annoyed
REFLECTION	3. Image as from a mirror
WHACKED	4. Struck, hit
GRUFFLY	5. Harshly
URGENT	6. Needing immediate action
BURLY	7. Husky
TIMIDLY	8. Hesitantly
LADEN	9. Burdened
MYSTIFIED	10. Bewildered, perplexed
BIASED	11. Prejudiced
DESPERATE	12. Nearly hopeless
CLOBBERED	13. Battered
PECULIAR	14. Odd, unusual
PELTING	15. Hurling
BLURTED	16. Said impulsively
TANTRUM	17. Fit
DESTINY	18. Fate
COWERING	19. Cringing
CLAMBERED	20. Climbed with difficulty

Sorcerer's Stone Vocabulary Fill In The Blank 4

_____ 1. Cringing

_____ 2. Moving gently

_____ 3. Turned suddenly

_____ 4. Scornful facial expression

_____ 5. Not allowed

_____ 6. Angrily

_____ 7. Cut, carved

_____ 8. Odd, unusual

_____ 9. Speaking unclearly

_____ 10. Disturbed, annoyed

_____ 11. Special medicine

_____ 12. Paralyzed with terror

_____ 13. Throw

_____ 14. Fired, let go

_____ 15. Annoyed

_____ 16. Meddling, bothering, in the way

_____ 17. Large kettle for boiling

_____ 18. Neat

_____ 19. Certain

_____ 20. Chubby, full in figure

Sorcerer's Stone Vocabulary Fill In The Blank 4 Answer Key

COWERING	1. Cringing
WAFTING	2. Moving gently
WHEELED	3. Turned suddenly
SNEER	4. Scornful facial expression
FORBIDDEN	5. Not allowed
FURIOUSLY	6. Angrily
WHITTLED	7. Cut, carved
PECULIAR	8. Odd, unusual
MUMBLING	9. Speaking unclearly
RUFFLED	10. Disturbed, annoyed
ELIXIR	11. Special medicine
PETRIFIED	12. Paralyzed with terror
FLING	13. Throw
SACKED	14. Fired, let go
MIFFED	15. Annoyed
INTERFERING	16. Meddling, bothering, in the way
CAULDRON	17. Large kettle for boiling
TIDY	18. Neat
CONVINCED	19. Certain
PLUMP	20. Chubby, full in figure

Sorcerer's Stone Vocabulary Matching 1

___ 1. KNACK A. Bewildered, perplexed
___ 2. MYSTIFIED B. Climbed with difficulty
___ 3. MUTELY C. Disturbed, annoyed
___ 4. TIMIDLY D. Stems, shoots
___ 5. AJAR E. Special talent
___ 6. FLING F. Throw
___ 7. FASCINATED G. Special medicine
___ 8. PETRIFIED H. Cringing
___ 9. PUB I. Tavern, bar
___10. ELIXIR J. Garbage, trash
___11. AMAZEMENT K. Intensely interested
___12. COWERING L. Regret
___13. CRANING M. Struggling
___14. FLINCHED N. Paralyzed with terror
___15. BLURTED O. Fit
___16. REMORSE P. Stretching, straining
___17. RUBBISH Q. Winced
___18. TANTRUM R. Angry frown
___19. SCOWL S. Said impulsively
___20. CLAMBERED T. Natural behavior
___21. RUFFLED U. Hesitantly
___22. GRAPPLING V. Wonder
___23. INSTINCT W. Partially open
___24. GOBLIN X. Grotesque elfin creature
___25. TENDRILS Y. Silently

Sorcerer's Stone Vocabulary Matching 1 Answer Key

E - 1. KNACK	A.	Bewildered, perplexed
A - 2. MYSTIFIED	B.	Climbed with difficulty
Y - 3. MUTELY	C.	Disturbed, annoyed
U - 4. TIMIDLY	D.	Stems, shoots
W - 5. AJAR	E.	Special talent
F - 6. FLING	F.	Throw
K - 7. FASCINATED	G.	Special medicine
N - 8. PETRIFIED	H.	Cringing
I - 9. PUB	I.	Tavern, bar
G - 10. ELIXIR	J.	Garbage, trash
V - 11. AMAZEMENT	K.	Intensely interested
H - 12. COWERING	L.	Regret
P - 13. CRANING	M.	Struggling
Q - 14. FLINCHED	N.	Paralyzed with terror
S - 15. BLURTED	O.	Fit
L - 16. REMORSE	P.	Stretching, straining
J - 17. RUBBISH	Q.	Winced
O - 18. TANTRUM	R.	Angry frown
R - 19. SCOWL	S.	Said impulsively
B - 20. CLAMBERED	T.	Natural behavior
C - 21. RUFFLED	U.	Hesitantly
M - 22. GRAPPLING	V.	Wonder
T - 23. INSTINCT	W.	Partially open
X - 24. GOBLIN	X.	Grotesque elfin creature
D - 25. TENDRILS	Y.	Silently

Sorcerer's Stone Vocabulary Matching 2

___ 1. DANGLING   A. Disturbed, annoyed
___ 2. GLEE   B. Foolish talk
___ 3. TIMIDLY   C. Prejudiced
___ 4. TANTRUM   D. Student officer
___ 5. SNIGGERED   E. Burst, spewed
___ 6. POLTERGEIST   F. Fit
___ 7. WHITTLED   G. Regret
___ 8. RUFFLED   H. Throw
___ 9. LINGERED   I. Delayed leaving
___10. TRODDEN   J. Joy
___11. ENORMOUS   K. Extreme pain
___12. REMORSE   L. Not allowed
___13. QUAILED   M. Burdened
___14. CLOBBERED   N. Very big
___15. BIASED   O. Walked on
___16. FORBIDDEN   P. Snickered
___17. ERUPTED   Q. Hanging loosely
___18. CONVINCED   R. Short strands of hair
___19. AGONY   S. Meddling, bothering, in the way
___20. PREFECT   T. Cut, carved
___21. LADEN   U. Hesitantly
___22. FLING   V. Battered
___23. BABBLE   W. Shrank in fear
___24. TUFTS   X. Certain
___25. INTERFERING   Y. Ghost that announces its presence

Sorcerer's Stone Vocabulary Matching 2 Answer Key

Q - 1. DANGLING		A. Disturbed, annoyed
J - 2. GLEE		B. Foolish talk
U - 3. TIMIDLY		C. Prejudiced
F - 4. TANTRUM		D. Student officer
P - 5. SNIGGERED		E. Burst, spewed
Y - 6. POLTERGEIST		F. Fit
T - 7. WHITTLED		G. Regret
A - 8. RUFFLED		H. Throw
I - 9. LINGERED		I. Delayed leaving
O -10. TRODDEN		J. Joy
N -11. ENORMOUS		K. Extreme pain
G -12. REMORSE		L. Not allowed
W -13. QUAILED		M. Burdened
V -14. CLOBBERED		N. Very big
C -15. BIASED		O. Walked on
L -16. FORBIDDEN		P. Snickered
E -17. ERUPTED		Q. Hanging loosely
X -18. CONVINCED		R. Short strands of hair
K -19. AGONY		S. Meddling, bothering, in the way
D -20. PREFECT		T. Cut, carved
M -21. LADEN		U. Hesitantly
H -22. FLING		V. Battered
B -23. BABBLE		W. Shrank in fear
R -24. TUFTS		X. Certain
S -25. INTERFERING		Y. Ghost that announces its presence

Copyrighted

Sorcerer's Stone Vocabulary Matching 3

___ 1. TUFTS   A. Hesitantly
___ 2. MUMBLING   B. Short strands of hair
___ 3. CLOAKS   C. Moving gently
___ 4. TIMIDLY   D. Loose outer garments
___ 5. GLOATINGLY   E. Snickered
___ 6. FEEBLE   F. Weak
___ 7. WAFTING   G. Stems, shoots
___ 8. TRODDEN   H. Tavern, bar
___ 9. EXPELLED   I. Cringing
___10. COWERING   J. In a self-satisfied way
___11. TANTRUM   K. Prejudiced
___12. SNEER   L. Extreme pain
___13. SNIGGERED   M. Scraping
___14. SCRABBLING   N. Forced, put out
___15. TENDRILS   O. Climbed with difficulty
___16. BIASED   P. Hurling
___17. PELTING   Q. Bewildered, perplexed
___18. DANGLING   R. Speaking unclearly
___19. CLAMBERED   S. Pushed, elbowed
___20. PUB   T. Needing immediate action
___21. MYSTIFIED   U. Scornful facial expression
___22. JOSTLED   V. Fit
___23. REMORSE   W. Hanging loosely
___24. URGENT   X. Regret
___25. AGONY   Y. Walked on

Sorcerer's Stone Vocabulary Matching 3 Answer Key

B - 1. TUFTS		A. Hesitantly
R - 2. MUMBLING		B. Short strands of hair
D - 3. CLOAKS		C. Moving gently
A - 4. TIMIDLY		D. Loose outer garments
J - 5. GLOATINGLY		E. Snickered
F - 6. FEEBLE		F. Weak
C - 7. WAFTING		G. Stems, shoots
Y - 8. TRODDEN		H. Tavern, bar
N - 9. EXPELLED		I. Cringing
I - 10. COWERING		J. In a self-satisfied way
V - 11. TANTRUM		K. Prejudiced
U - 12. SNEER		L. Extreme pain
E - 13. SNIGGERED		M. Scraping
M - 14. SCRABBLING		N. Forced, put out
G - 15. TENDRILS		O. Climbed with difficulty
K - 16. BIASED		P. Hurling
P - 17. PELTING		Q. Bewildered, perplexed
W - 18. DANGLING		R. Speaking unclearly
O - 19. CLAMBERED		S. Pushed, elbowed
H - 20. PUB		T. Needing immediate action
Q - 21. MYSTIFIED		U. Scornful facial expression
S - 22. JOSTLED		V. Fit
X - 23. REMORSE		W. Hanging loosely
T - 24. URGENT		X. Regret
L - 25. AGONY		Y. Walked on

Sorcerer's Stone Vocabulary Matching 4

___ 1. DESTINY   A. Forced, put out
___ 2. POLTERGEIST   B. Ghost that announces its presence
___ 3. QUAILED   C. Struggling
___ 4. MUMBLING   D. Speaking unclearly
___ 5. FEEBLE   E. Very shocked
___ 6. PELTING   F. Struck, hit
___ 7. HITCH   G. In a self-satisfied way
___ 8. EXPELLED   H. Witches
___ 9. GOGGLE   I. Weak
___10. GRAPPLING   J. Burdened
___11. CLOBBERED   K. Winced
___12. FLINCHED   L. Sign
___13. AMAZEMENT   M. Chubby, full in figure
___14. HORRIFIED   N. Fate
___15. GLOATINGLY   O. Delay
___16. CLOAKS   P. Stare
___17. CAULDRON   Q. Angry frown
___18. SEIZED   R. Hurling
___19. PLUMP   S. Dunce, dummy
___20. LADEN   T. Loose outer garments
___21. OMEN   U. Battered
___22. HAGS   V. Wonder
___23. WHACKED   W. Shrank in fear
___24. SCOWL   X. Large kettle for boiling
___25. DUNDERHEAD   Y. Grabbed

Sorcerer's Stone Vocabulary Matching 4 Answer Key

N - 1. DESTINY	A.	Forced, put out
B - 2. POLTERGEIST	B.	Ghost that announces its presence
W - 3. QUAILED	C.	Struggling
D - 4. MUMBLING	D.	Speaking unclearly
I - 5. FEEBLE	E.	Very shocked
R - 6. PELTING	F.	Struck, hit
O - 7. HITCH	G.	In a self-satisfied way
A - 8. EXPELLED	H.	Witches
P - 9. GOGGLE	I.	Weak
C - 10. GRAPPLING	J.	Burdened
U - 11. CLOBBERED	K.	Winced
K - 12. FLINCHED	L.	Sign
V - 13. AMAZEMENT	M.	Chubby, full in figure
E - 14. HORRIFIED	N.	Fate
G - 15. GLOATINGLY	O.	Delay
T - 16. CLOAKS	P.	Stare
X - 17. CAULDRON	Q.	Angry frown
Y - 18. SEIZED	R.	Hurling
M - 19. PLUMP	S.	Dunce, dummy
J - 20. LADEN	T.	Loose outer garments
L - 21. OMEN	U.	Battered
H - 22. HAGS	V.	Wonder
F - 23. WHACKED	W.	Shrank in fear
Q - 24. SCOWL	X.	Large kettle for boiling
S - 25. DUNDERHEAD	Y.	Grabbed

Sorcerer's Stone Vocabulary Magic Squares 1

Match the definition with the vocabulary word. Put your answers in the magic squares below. When your answers are correct, all columns and rows will add to the same number.

A. SNEER
B. SCRABBLING
C. MYSTIFIED
D. FLINCHED
E. TUFTS
F. SNIGGERED
G. AJAR
H. DESPERATE
I. AMAZEMENT
J. INTERFERING
K. BIASED
L. SPECTACLES
M. RUBBISH
N. ENORMOUS
O. PREFECT
P. SACKED

1. Very big
2. Partially open
3. Glasses
4. Scornful facial expression
5. Prejudiced
6. Scraping
7. Garbage, trash
8. Nearly hopeless
9. Short strands of hair
10. Fired, let go
11. Bewildered, perplexed
12. Meddling, bothering, in the way
13. Winced
14. Wonder
15. Snickered
16. Student officer

A=	B=	C=	D=
E=	F=	G=	H=
I=	J=	K=	L=
M=	N=	O=	P=

Sorcerer's Stone Vocabulary Magic Squares 1 Answer Key

Match the definition with the vocabulary word. Put your answers in the magic squares below. When your answers are correct, all columns and rows will add to the same number.

A. SNEER
B. SCRABBLING
C. MYSTIFIED
D. FLINCHED
E. TUFTS
F. SNIGGERED
G. AJAR
H. DESPERATE
I. AMAZEMENT
J. INTERFERING
K. BIASED
L. SPECTACLES
M. RUBBISH
N. ENORMOUS
O. PREFECT
P. SACKED

1. Very big
2. Partially open
3. Glasses
4. Scornful facial expression
5. Prejudiced
6. Scraping
7. Garbage, trash
8. Nearly hopeless
9. Short strands of hair
10. Fired, let go
11. Bewildered, perplexed
12. Meddling, bothering, in the way
13. Winced
14. Wonder
15. Snickered
16. Student officer

A=4	B=6	C=11	D=13
E=9	F=15	G=2	H=8
I=14	J=12	K=5	L=3
M=7	N=1	O=16	P=10

Sorcerer's Stone Vocabulary Magic Squares 2

Match the definition with the vocabulary word. Put your answers in the magic squares below. When your answers are correct, all columns and rows will add to the same number.

A. GLISTENING
B. FLING
C. SNEER
D. SAVAGING
E. SHUDDERED
F. GOBLIN
G. DANGLING
H. WIZARD
I. TIMIDLY
J. BABBLE
K. CRANING
L. OMEN
M. BIASED
N. MANGLED
O. MYSTIFIED
P. ENORMOUS

1. Magician
2. Glittering
3. Throw
4. Hanging loosely
5. Foolish talk
6. Bewildered, perplexed
7. Very big
8. Hesitantly
9. Stretching, straining
10. Torn, mutilated
11. Prejudiced
12. Sign
13. Shivered, as from fear or aversion
14. Attacking violently
15. Scornful facial expression
16. Grotesque elfin creature

A=	B=	C=	D=
E=	F=	G=	H=
I=	J=	K=	L=
M=	N=	O=	P=

Sorcerer's Stone Vocabulary Magic Squares 2 Answer Key

Match the definition with the vocabulary word. Put your answers in the magic squares below. When your answers are correct, all columns and rows will add to the same number.

A. GLISTENING
B. FLING
C. SNEER
D. SAVAGING
E. SHUDDERED
F. GOBLIN
G. DANGLING
H. WIZARD
I. TIMIDLY
J. BABBLE
K. CRANING
L. OMEN
M. BIASED
N. MANGLED
O. MYSTIFIED
P. ENORMOUS

1. Magician
2. Glittering
3. Throw
4. Hanging loosely
5. Foolish talk
6. Bewildered, perplexed
7. Very big
8. Hesitantly
9. Stretching, straining
10. Torn, mutilated
11. Prejudiced
12. Sign
13. Shivered, as from fear or aversion
14. Attacking violently
15. Scornful facial expression
16. Grotesque elfin creature

A=2	B=3	C=15	D=14
E=13	F=16	G=4	H=1
I=8	J=5	K=9	L=12
M=11	N=10	O=6	P=7

Sorcerer's Stone Vocabulary Magic Squares 3

Match the definition with the vocabulary word. Put your answers in the magic squares below. When your answers are correct, all columns and rows will add to the same number.

A. TANTRUM
B. PLUMP
C. SPECTACLES
D. LINGERED
E. DESPERATE
F. FLINCHED
G. ELIXIR
H. GLOOMY
I. WAFTING
J. PELTING
K. REFLECTION
L. TIDY
M. CLOBBERED
N. WIZARD
O. TENDRILS
P. CAULDRON

1. Chubby, full in figure
2. Special medicine
3. Image as from a mirror
4. Magician
5. Battered
6. Neat
7. Dark, dreary
8. Fit
9. Large kettle for boiling
10. Moving gently
11. Nearly hopeless
12. Delayed leaving
13. Glasses
14. Winced
15. Hurling
16. Stems, shoots

A=	B=	C=	D=
E=	F=	G=	H=
I=	J=	K=	L=
M=	N=	O=	P=

Sorcerer's Stone Vocabulary Magic Squares 3 Answer Key

Match the definition with the vocabulary word. Put your answers in the magic squares below. When your answers are correct, all columns and rows will add to the same number.

A. TANTRUM
B. PLUMP
C. SPECTACLES
D. LINGERED
E. DESPERATE
F. FLINCHED
G. ELIXIR
H. GLOOMY
I. WAFTING
J. PELTING
K. REFLECTION
L. TIDY
M. CLOBBERED
N. WIZARD
O. TENDRILS
P. CAULDRON

1. Chubby, full in figure
2. Special medicine
3. Image as from a mirror
4. Magician
5. Battered
6. Neat
7. Dark, dreary
8. Fit
9. Large kettle for boiling
10. Moving gently
11. Nearly hopeless
12. Delayed leaving
13. Glasses
14. Winced
15. Hurling
16. Stems, shoots

A=8	B=1	C=13	D=12
E=11	F=14	G=2	H=7
I=10	J=15	K=3	L=6
M=5	N=4	O=16	P=9

Copyrighted

Sorcerer's Stone Vocabulary Magic Squares 4

Match the definition with the vocabulary word. Put your answers in the magic squares below. When your answers are correct, all columns and rows will add to the same number.

A. GOGGLE
B. OMEN
C. CLOAKS
D. SLITHER
E. SUPPOSED
F. GOBLIN
G. DUNDERHEAD
H. LADEN
I. TUFTS
J. FLING
K. MYSTIFIED
L. SEIZED
M. WHACKED
N. WAFTING
O. SNIGGERED
P. INTERFERING

1. Snickered
2. Slide, glide
3. Throw
4. Assumed to be true
5. Short strands of hair
6. Grotesque elfin creature
7. Meddling, bothering, in the way
8. Loose outer garments
9. Burdened
10. Bewildered, perplexed
11. Stare
12. Moving gently
13. Sign
14. Struck, hit
15. Dunce, dummy
16. Grabbed

A=	B=	C=	D=
E=	F=	G=	H=
I=	J=	K=	L=
M=	N=	O=	P=

85
Copyrighted

Sorcerer's Stone Vocabulary Magic Squares 4 Answer Key

Match the definition with the vocabulary word. Put your answers in the magic squares below. When your answers are correct, all columns and rows will add to the same number.

A. GOGGLE
B. OMEN
C. CLOAKS
D. SLITHER
E. SUPPOSED
F. GOBLIN
G. DUNDERHEAD
H. LADEN
I. TUFTS
J. FLING
K. MYSTIFIED
L. SEIZED
M. WHACKED
N. WAFTING
O. SNIGGERED
P. INTERFERING

1. Snickered
2. Slide, glide
3. Throw
4. Assumed to be true
5. Short strands of hair
6. Grotesque elfin creature
7. Meddling, bothering, in the way
8. Loose outer garments
9. Burdened
10. Bewildered, perplexed
11. Stare
12. Moving gently
13. Sign
14. Struck, hit
15. Dunce, dummy
16. Grabbed

A=11	B=13	C=8	D=2
E=4	F=6	G=15	H=9
I=5	J=3	K=10	L=16
M=14	N=12	O=1	P=7

Sorcerer's Stone Vocabulary Word Search 1

```
P D F H O R R I F I E D B R M U T E L Y
E E T E K M G C D R E X E U R V E L I N
T L C H E N E E X I G F N F R L H I N K
R E W U I B L N F C L R V F G L M X G P
I E F L L I L I S E E E I L C L Y I E V
F H F T A I T E C T G H N E L W V R R Z
I W N U P S A T S N O T T D O O V B E Q
E D Q H Y N I R S M B I E S A C K E D Z
D R E M H O P Y L L L R P K S R L K Y
L Y U S N Y H O U C I S F L S F E B N C
W F S P T L S R L F N G E U K U M B D P
R A T C T I T N P T G A R M B R O A N L
F S E F R E N I I W E H I P U Y R B A D
T C N K D D Y D G F R N R X S S D E T
I I D D N A G O N Y G O G L E E L V Y
M N R H S A Q Z M N X E R E Y N L Q S F
I A I A I P C O K D N E R Q I E P T K Y
D T L J T T O K N T E F R E P S F L L F
L E S A H L C R A N I N G X D U T P U B
Y D M R G J G H S R S P E C T A C L E S
```

Angry frown (5)
Bewildered, perplexed (9)
Burdened (5)
Burst, spewed (7)
Chubby, full in figure (5)
Dark, dreary (6)
Delay (5)
Delayed leaving (8)
Disturbed, annoyed (7)
Extreme pain (5)
Fate (7)
Fired, let go (6)
Firm, severe (5)
Foolish talk (6)
Forced, put out (8)
Ghost that announces its presence (11)
Glasses (10)
Grotesque elfin creature (6)
Hesitantly (7)
Husky (5)
Image as from a mirror (10)
Intense anger, rage (4)
Intensely interested (10)
Joy (4)
Loose outer garments (6)
Meddling, bothering, in the way (11)

Neat (4)
Needing immediate action (6)
Odd, unusual (8)
Paralyzed with terror (9)
Partially open (4)
Regret (7)
Said impulsively (7)
Scornful facial expression (5)
Short strands of hair (5)
Shrank in fear (7)
Sign (4)
Silently (6)
Slide, glide (7)
Snickered (9)
Special medicine (6)
Special talent (5)
Stare (6)
Stems, shoots (8)
Stretching, straining (7)
Tavern, bar (3)
Throw (5)
Turned suddenly (7)
Very shocked (9)
Weak (6)
Witches (4)

Sorcerer's Stone Vocabulary Word Search 1 Answer Key

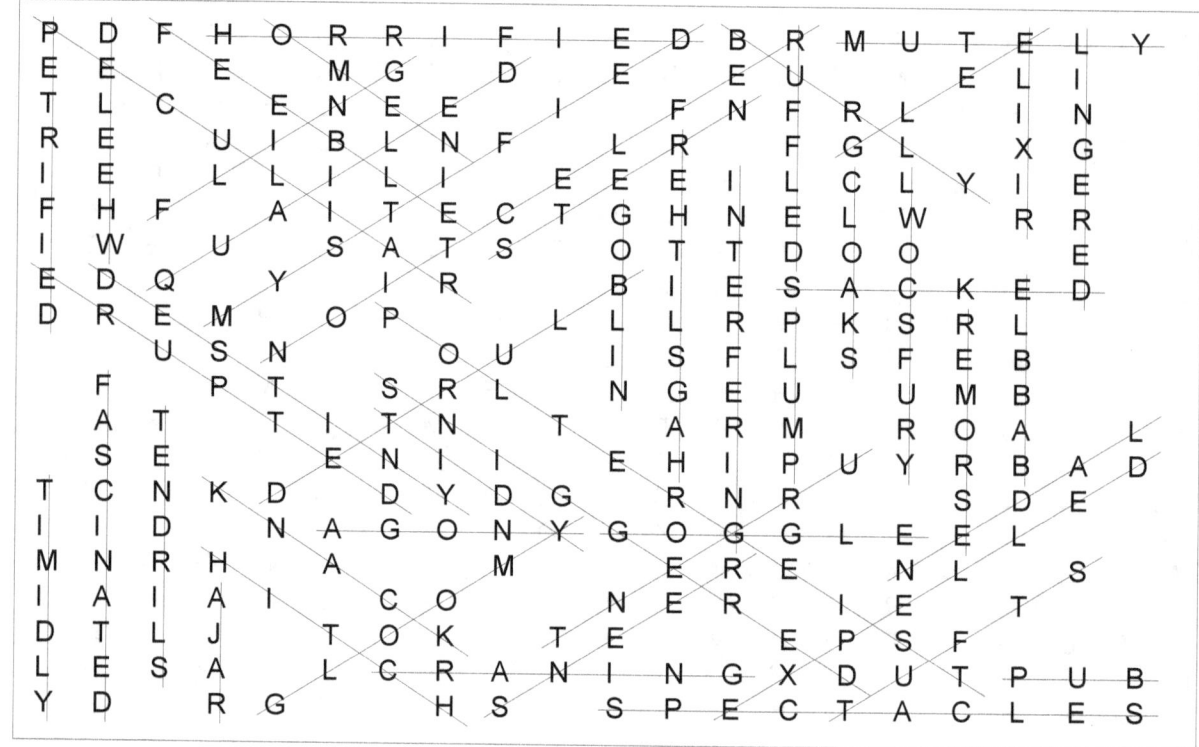

Angry frown (5)
Bewildered, perplexed (9)
Burdened (5)
Burst, spewed (7)
Chubby, full in figure (5)
Dark, dreary (6)
Delay (5)
Delayed leaving (8)
Disturbed, annoyed (7)
Extreme pain (5)
Fate (7)
Fired, let go (6)
Firm, severe (5)
Foolish talk (6)
Forced, put out (8)
Ghost that announces its presence (11)
Glasses (10)
Grotesque elfin creature (6)
Hesitantly (7)
Husky (5)
Image as from a mirror (10)
Intense anger, rage (4)
Intensely interested (10)
Joy (4)
Loose outer garments (6)
Meddling, bothering, in the way (11)

Neat (4)
Needing immediate action (6)
Odd, unusual (8)
Paralyzed with terror (9)
Partially open (4)
Regret (7)
Said impulsively (7)
Scornful facial expression (5)
Short strands of hair (5)
Shrank in fear (7)
Sign (4)
Silently (6)
Slide, glide (7)
Snickered (9)
Special medicine (6)
Special talent (5)
Stare (6)
Stems, shoots (8)
Stretching, straining (7)
Tavern, bar (3)
Throw (5)
Turned suddenly (7)
Very shocked (9)
Weak (6)
Witches (4)

Sorcerer's Stone Vocabulary Word Search 2

```
K S E I Z E D E R E B B O L C A G O N Y
N D R A Z I W A N P R F F W E M N S N N
I J U P B H J D N O L J X O T A I T Y C
C K P G E A E S G G R U X C A Z N F N L
K H T Z E L B E E F L M M S R E A U N S
E H E M K P T N M D C I O P E M R T G N
R O D N C Z B I T H Y A N U P E C N O N
B R I P O V F C N R Z S U G S N C E G S
O R D C W F E C U G K Z T L E T L G G C
C I O M E N L F L I N C H E D B U R L Y
K F R D R J I A H B A B D E K R A U E V
E I E C I Q X S I X C S K H L P O X F C
R E E L N U I C T J K C H G P F S N K G
S D N B G A R I C Y A D E L L E P X E S
M H S L O I D N H H M X I I A O Z R A B
Q S K U B L P A W U A N N W D S O C W S
S N A R L E D T T W G G V J E T K M B W
K N O T I D P E I N C L S H N E M U Y T
N X L E N W L D D J J E W J D R P Y P G
N B C D F Y Y S Y B L E Y T A N T R U M
```

Angry frown (5)
Annoyed (6)
Battered (9)
Burdened (5)
Burst, spewed (7)
Chubby, full in figure (5)
Cringing (8)
Dark, dreary (6)
Delay (5)
Extreme pain (5)
Fired, let go (6)
Firm, severe (5)
Fit (7)
Forced, put out (8)
Full pants gathered below the knee (14)
Grabbed (6)
Grotesque elfin creature (6)
Growled (7)
Hanging loosely (8)
Hurling (7)
Husky (5)
Intense anger, rage (4)
Intensely interested (10)
Joy (4)
Large kettle for boiling (8)
Loose outer garments (6)

Magician (6)
Nearly hopeless (9)
Neat (4)
Needing immediate action (6)
Partially open (4)
Said impulsively (7)
Scornful facial expression (5)
Short strands of hair (5)
Shrank in fear (7)
Sign (4)
Silently (6)
Special medicine (6)
Special talent (5)
Stare (6)
Stretching, straining (7)
Struck, hit (7)
Struggling (9)
Tavern, bar (3)
Throw (5)
Very big (8)
Very shocked (9)
Weak (6)
Winced (8)
Witches (4)
Wonder (9)
Wrinkled (8)

Sorcerer's Stone Vocabulary Word Search 2 Asnwer Key

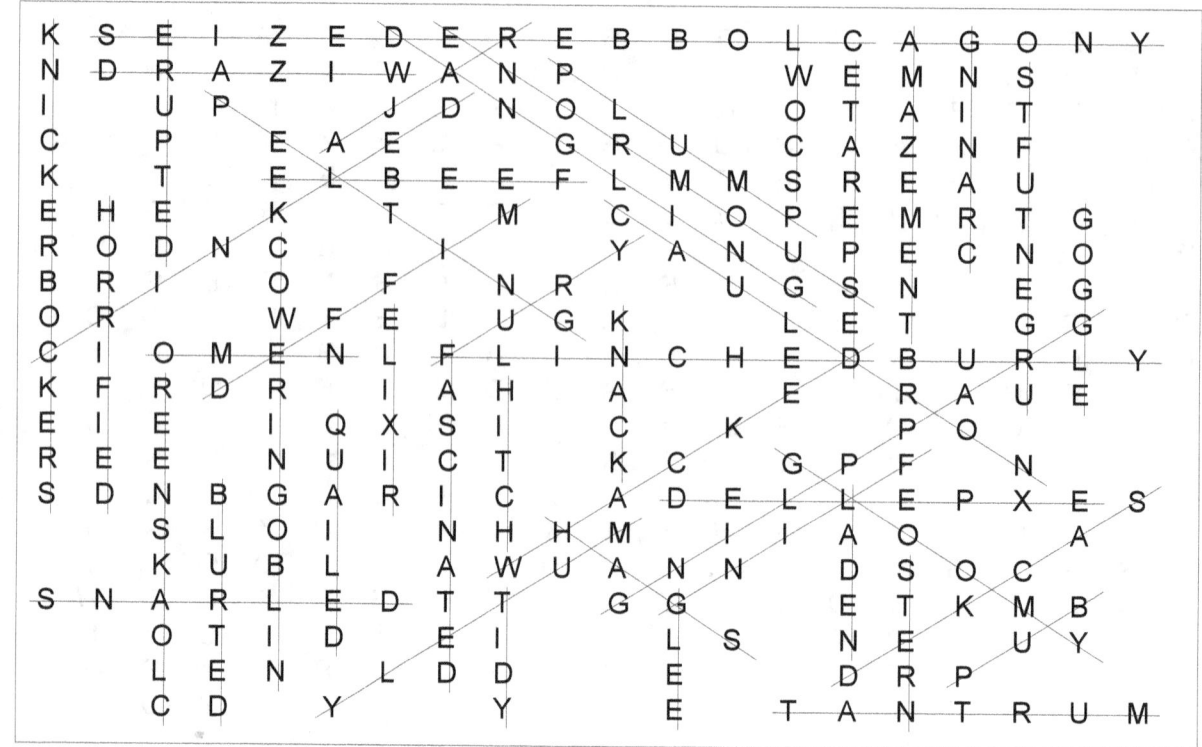

Angry frown (5)
Annoyed (6)
Battered (9)
Burdened (5)
Burst, spewed (7)
Chubby, full in figure (5)
Cringing (8)
Dark, dreary (6)
Delay (5)
Extreme pain (5)
Fired, let go (6)
Firm, severe (5)
Fit (7)
Forced, put out (8)
Full pants gathered below the knee (14)
Grabbed (6)
Grotesque elfin creature (6)
Growled (7)
Hanging loosely (8)
Hurling (7)
Husky (5)
Intense anger, rage (4)
Intensely interested (10)
Joy (4)
Large kettle for boiling (8)
Loose outer garments (6)

Magician (6)
Nearly hopeless (9)
Neat (4)
Needing immediate action (6)
Partially open (4)
Said impulsively (7)
Scornful facial expression (5)
Short strands of hair (5)
Shrank in fear (7)
Sign (4)
Silently (6)
Special medicine (6)
Special talent (5)
Stare (6)
Stretching, straining (7)
Struck, hit (7)
Struggling (9)
Tavern, bar (3)
Throw (5)
Very big (8)
Very shocked (9)
Weak (6)
Winced (8)
Witches (4)
Wonder (9)
Wrinkled (8)

90
Copyrighted

Sorcerer's Stone Vocabulary Word Search 3

```
F W H E E L E D E Q D E S O P P U S B W
U S C R P M D X Q L Z E Z Z W Q U N U V
R A L U X V X P T I Y S Z F O A A R V
Y C O P N U G G D E N X T P M Q J R L S
W K A T T E N D R I L S I R E G A L Y V
I E K E C I I D T A G L O R O R R E L L
Z D S D R W R S E A P N E G U D A D O Q
A F N E P G E E H R E P G D R G D T M Z
R W V G T D W H F G H L L N G D N E E G
D O H N A Y O S L L E R I E L Q S N X
H N P I N B C O I H E E A F N C O R G R
W V B N T Q J L N A T C F D T G R O C B
L U G A R T C A C S G I T Y K U H M M P
P Y K R U S L G H T M O L I B V C E S Y
J K P C M N B E E W U F N B O F Q R W B
M N H C T I H S D L R F I Y C N L Q A J
N A N D A G W Q M U H S T Y D I T B D D
C C N S D G V B F U H N Z S N E B M E G
Z K E G F E C F N D T E E G Q L T Z L C
T D J T L R L K I F N E E P E B I S F Y
T B V K P E C U L I A R L A D E N C F J
K Z D B D D I B Z E U G Y S E R O U M
M U M B L I N G O D M G N I T F A W H V
N S A V A G I N G P T I M I D L Y L S C
```

AGONY	ERUPTED	HITCH	REFLECTION	SUPPOSED
AJAR	EXPELLED	HOVERING	REMORSE	TANTRUM
BABBLE	FEEBLE	KNACK	RUBBISH	TENDRILS
BIASED	FLINCHED	LADEN	RUFFLED	TIDY
BURLY	FLING	LINGERED	SACKED	TIMIDLY
CLOAKS	FURY	MANGLED	SAVAGING	TRODDEN
COWERING	GALOSHES	MIFFED	SCOWL	TUFTS
CRANING	GLEE	MUMBLING	SEIZED	URGENT
DESPERATE	GLOOMY	MUTELY	SHUFFLED	WAFTING
DESTINY	GOBLIN	OMEN	SNARLED	WHEELED
DUNDERHEAD	GOGGLE	PECULIAR	SNEER	WHITTLED
ELIXIR	GRAPPLING	PLUMP	SNIGGERED	WIZARD
ENORMOUS	HAGS	PUB	STERN	

Sorcerer's Stone Vocabulary Word Search 3 Answer Key

AGONY	ERUPTED	HITCH	REFLECTION	SUPPOSED
AJAR	EXPELLED	HOVERING	REMORSE	TANTRUM
BABBLE	FEEBLE	KNACK	RUBBISH	TENDRILS
BIASED	FLINCHED	LADEN	RUFFLED	TIDY
BURLY	FLING	LINGERED	SACKED	TIMIDLY
CLOAKS	FURY	MANGLED	SAVAGING	TRODDEN
COWERING	GALOSHES	MIFFED	SCOWL	TUFTS
CRANING	GLEE	MUMBLING	SEIZED	URGENT
DESPERATE	GLOOMY	MUTELY	SHUFFLED	WAFTING
DESTINY	GOBLIN	OMEN	SNARLED	WHEELED
DUNDERHEAD	GOGGLE	PECULIAR	SNEER	WHITTLED
ELIXIR	GRAPPLING	PLUMP	SNIGGERED	WIZARD
ENORMOUS	HAGS	PUB	STERN	

Sorcerer's Stone Vocabulary Word Search 4

```
K N A C K C M A N G L E D S E L I X I R
F L I N G T A G V S D Q Q W A V P C X K
M U T E G T Y X U L H U J W H A C K E D M
L R U F L Y E D L V K P L N V F K D S R
F A S C F L N A T E D E S P E R A T E T Y
F I D Y I N B J E E R P N O P B I I D Q
P L R E X N R N L T O T E S Y M F N R
F U F C D B E M E T C L N V E I I J G
F C B V N E S L M S A T E Y V R D R C P
Y E X D B G T O O J E G P T U L R H H
Y P O A L E L I J A R R D Z P Y O G R
S R L F E N B S X N R G U H I T C H N C
T C G G O I O U P N Y E A K Y E C I I W
E P N R Y L K R R E Q I X L B D L N T F
R C I G N B Q C M L C S B L O B V Z L L
N L R L P M U L P O Y T U A O S Y X E F
S W E I L U G O Q E U R A G B D H L P S
W I V S N M N A H F T S P C I B B E A Y
H Z O T B K I K T E J R S T L E L V S M
E A H E I X L S D S Y P I E E E A I K
E R A N A B G E B C N G E F I G S F L M
L D G I S C N D O O L P W I Z F K P L
E P S N E Z A G G W G S X N F E E S C C
D D J G D H D D S L A B G M D W D D K V
```

AGONY	ELIXIR	HITCH	PETRIFIED	TENDRILS
AJAR	ENORMOUS	HORRIFIED	PLUMP	TIDY
BABBLE	ERUPTED	HOVERING	POLTERGEIST	TIMIDLY
BIASED	FASCINATED	JOSTLED	PUB	TRODDEN
BLURTED	FEEBLE	KNACK	RUFFLED	TUFTS
BURLY	FLING	LADEN	SACKED	URGENT
CAULDRON	FURY	MANGLED	SAVAGING	WAFTING
CLAMBERED	GALOSHES	MIFFED	SCOWL	WHACKED
CLOAKS	GLEE	MUMBLING	SEIZED	WHEELED
CRINKLED	GLISTENING	MUTELY	SNEER	WIZARD
DANGLING	GOBLIN	OMEN	SPECTACLES	
DESPERATE	GOGGLE	PECULIAR	STERN	
DESTINY	HAGS	PELTING	SUPPOSED	

Sorcerer's Stone Vocabulary Word Search 4 Answer Key

```
K N A C K C M A N G L E D S E L I X I R
  F L I N G   A       S         W A
  M U T E L Y   U       U     W H A C K E D
  L R U F F L E D L     P         F K D
  F A S C I N A T E D E S P E R A T E D
      I   D       E E   P N O   T I   N
    P L   R   D   N R   L T   E   M F   G
      U   E   N   D E   T N   S   E I
    F C B   D B S L M   E E   E   R R
      E   D A M E E T O   G   R U D R
      P O A O N B S   J   R   U P L O
    S R C G G D I O P N   U   P T Y G N
    T   N R   L U R M E   I   H I   I
    E   C I   B R C P L   S   E   C T
    R   L   G   C     O   T   D   H L
    N   W   R   L     Y B U A   L B O E
    S   I   E   L     U R A G B D S Y P S
    W   Z   V   I     T S C B B H L E A
    H   A   E   S     T I L E V S M
    E   R       L     E R I E I
    E   D       H     D     F G F
    L                   S     Z E E D
    E                                   D
    D
```

AGONY	ELIXIR	HITCH	PETRIFIED	TENDRILS
AJAR	ENORMOUS	HORRIFIED	PLUMP	TIDY
BABBLE	ERUPTED	HOVERING	POLTERGEIST	TIMIDLY
BIASED	FASCINATED	JOSTLED	PUB	TRODDEN
BLURTED	FEEBLE	KNACK	RUFFLED	TUFTS
BURLY	FLING	LADEN	SACKED	URGENT
CAULDRON	FURY	MANGLED	SAVAGING	WAFTING
CLAMBERED	GALOSHES	MIFFED	SCOWL	WHACKED
CLOAKS	GLEE	MUMBLING	SEIZED	WHEELED
CRINKLED	GLISTENING	MUTELY	SNEER	WIZARD
DANGLING	GOBLIN	OMEN	SPECTACLES	
DESPERATE	GOGGLE	PECULIAR	STERN	
DESTINY	HAGS	PELTING	SUPPOSED	

Sorcerer's Stone Vocabulary Crossword 1

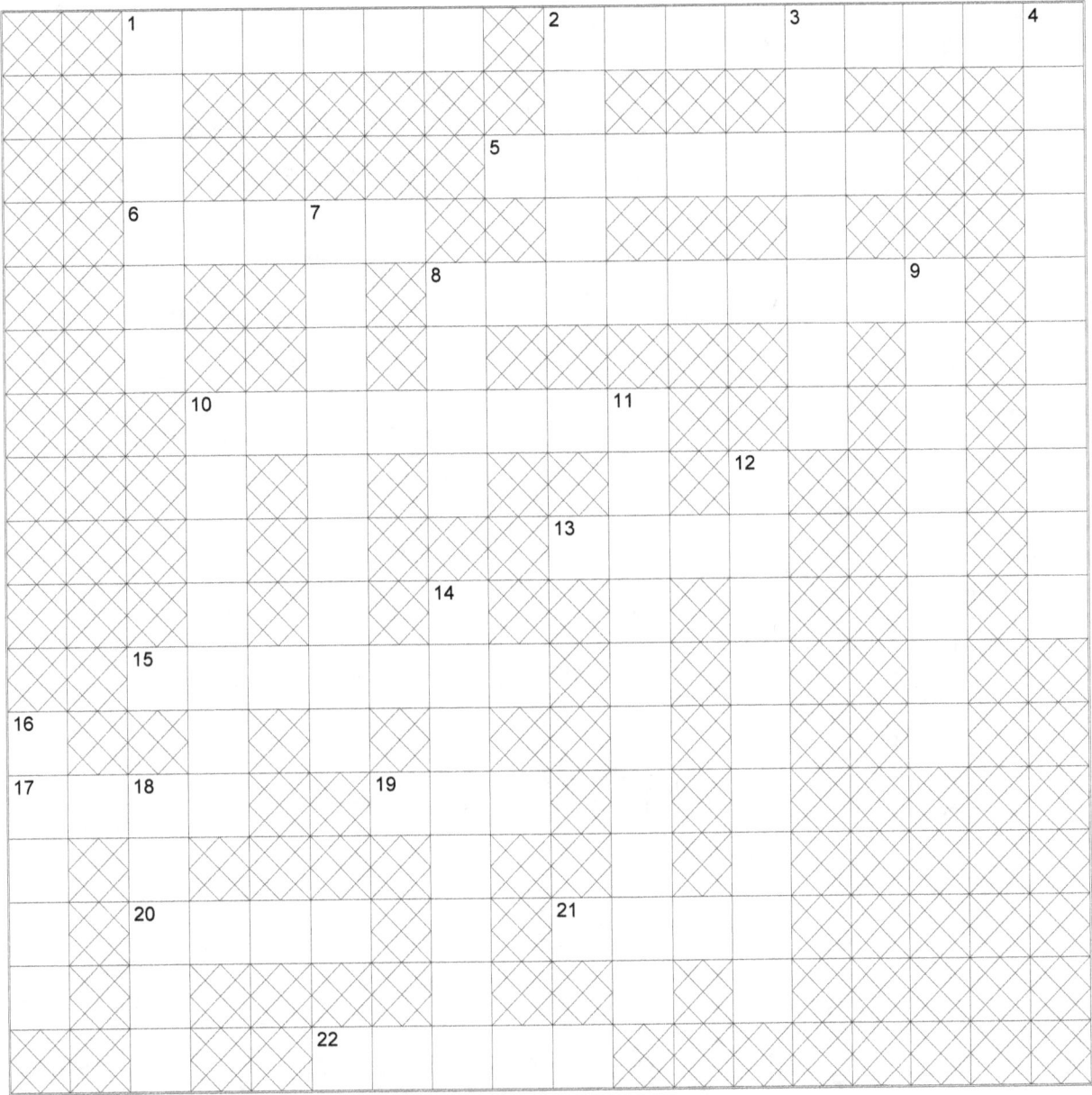

Across
1. Grabbed
2. Shivered, as from fear or aversion
5. Regret
6. Special talent
8. Very shocked
10. Attacking violently
13. Intense anger, rage
15. Turned suddenly
17. Partially open
19. Tavern, bar
20. Sign
21. Joy
22. Husky

Down
1. Fired, let go
2. Scornful facial expression
3. Fate
4. Dunce, dummy
7. Certain
8. Witches
9. Hanging loosely
10. Slide, glide
11. Reluctantly
12. Bewildered, perplexed
14. Odd, unusual
16. Burdened
18. Extreme pain

Sorcerer's Stone Vocabulary Crossword 1 Answer Key

	1 S	E	I	Z	E	D		2 S	H	U	3 D	D	E	R	E	4 D
	A							N			E					U
	C					5 R	E	M	O	R	S	E				N
	6 K	N	A	7 C	K			E			T					D
	E			O			8 H	O	R	R	I	F	I	E	9 D	E
	D			N			A				N				A	R
			10 S	A	V	A	G	I	11 N	G			Y		N	H
			L		I		S		R		12 M				G	E
			I		N			13 F	U	R	Y				L	A
			T		C		14 P		D		S				I	D
		15 W	H	E	E	L	E	D		G		T			N	
	16 L		E		D		C			I		I			G	
	17 A	18 J	A	R		19 P	U	B		N		F				
	D	G					L			G		I				
	E	20 O	M	E	N		I		21 G	L	E	E				
	N	N					A		Y		D					
		Y		22 B	U	R	L	Y								

Across
1. Grabbed
2. Shivered, as from fear or aversion
5. Regret
6. Special talent
8. Very shocked
10. Attacking violently
13. Intense anger, rage
15. Turned suddenly
17. Partially open
19. Tavern, bar
20. Sign
21. Joy
22. Husky

Down
1. Fired, let go

2. Scornful facial expression
3. Fate
4. Dunce, dummy
7. Certain
8. Witches
9. Hanging loosely
10. Slide, glide
11. Reluctantly
12. Bewildered, perplexed
14. Odd, unusual
16. Burdened
18. Extreme pain

Sorcerer's Stone Vocabulary Crossword 2

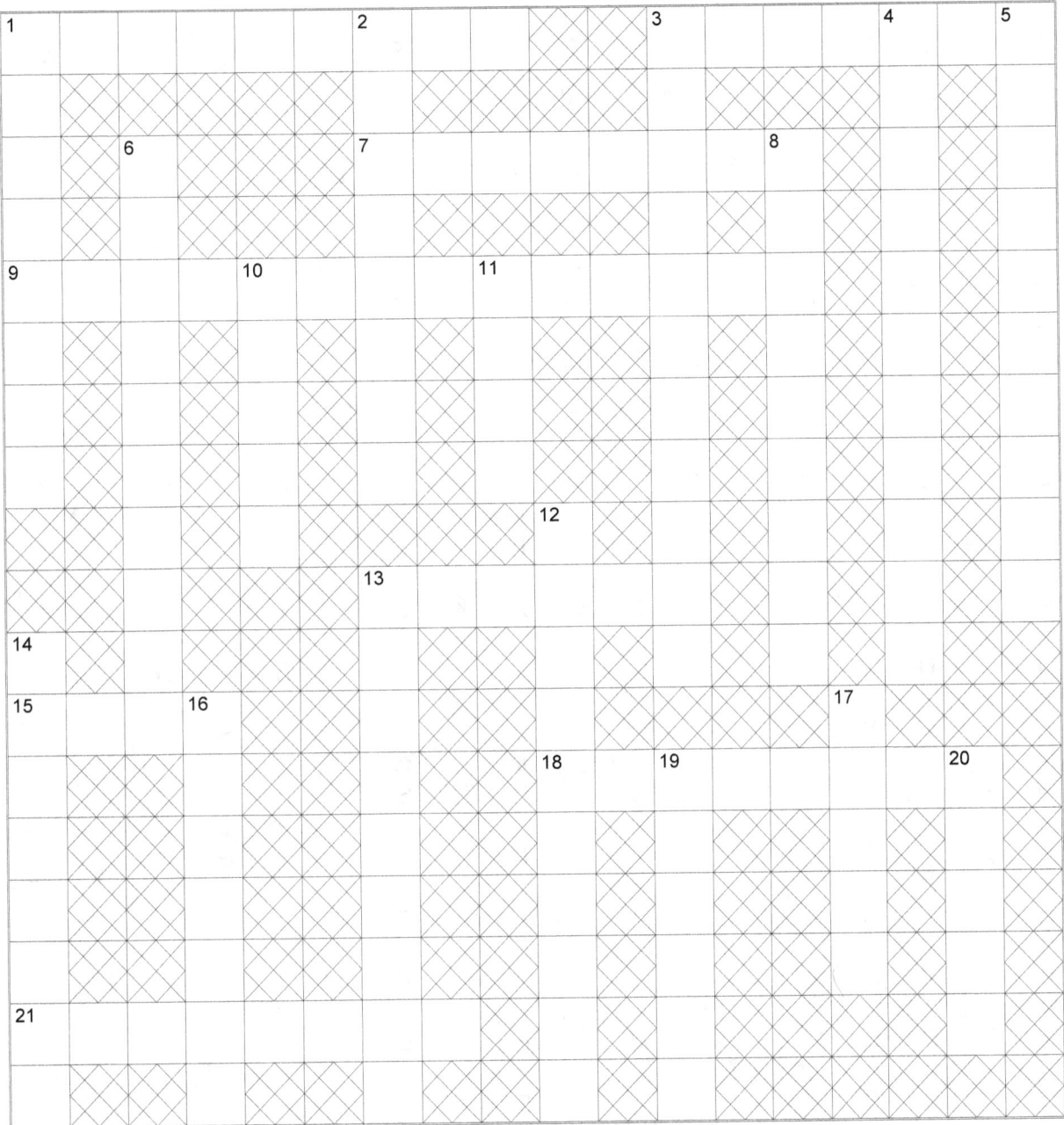

Across
1. Certain
3. Hurling
7. Cut, carved
9. Full pants gathered below the knee
13. Loose outer garments
15. Witches
18. Natural behavior
21. Forced, put out

Down
1. Wrinkled
2. Cringing
3. Ghost that announces its presence
4. Meddling, bothering, in the way
5. In a self-satisfied way
6. Glittering
8. Nearly hopeless
10. Special talent
11. Sign
12. Intensely interested
13. Battered
14. Walked while dragging feet
16. Growled
17. Scornful facial expression
19. Fired, let go
20. Short strands of hair

Sorcerer's Stone Vocabulary Crossword 2 Answer Key

	1 C	O	N	V	I	N	2 C	E	D		3 P	E	L	T	4 I	N	5 G
	R						O				O				N		L
	I		6 G			7 W	H	I	T	T	L	E	8 D		T		O
	N		L			E				T			E		E		A
	9 K	N	I	10 C	K	E	R	B	11 O	C	K	E	R	S		R		T
	L		S		N		I		M			R		P		F		I
	E		T		A		N		E			G		E		E		N
	D		E		C		G		N			E		R		R		G
			N		K				12 F			I		A		I		L
			I			13 C	L	O	A	K	S		T		N		Y
14 S		N				L			S			T		E		G		
15 H	A	G	16 S			O			C					17 S			
U			N			B			18 I	19 N	S	T	I	N	C	20 T	
F			A			B			N		A			E		U	
F			R			E			A		C			E		F	
L			L			R			T		K			R		T	
21 E	X	P	E	L	L	E	D		E		E					S	
D			D			D			D		D						

Across
1. Certain
3. Hurling
7. Cut, carved
9. Full pants gathered below the knee
13. Loose outer garments
15. Witches
18. Natural behavior
21. Forced, put out

Down
1. Wrinkled
2. Cringing
3. Ghost that announces its presence
4. Meddling, bothering, in the way
5. In a self-satisfied way
6. Glittering
8. Nearly hopeless
10. Special talent
11. Sign
12. Intensely interested
13. Battered
14. Walked while dragging feet
16. Growled
17. Scornful facial expression
19. Fired, let go
20. Short strands of hair

Sorcerer's Stone Vocabulary Crossword 3

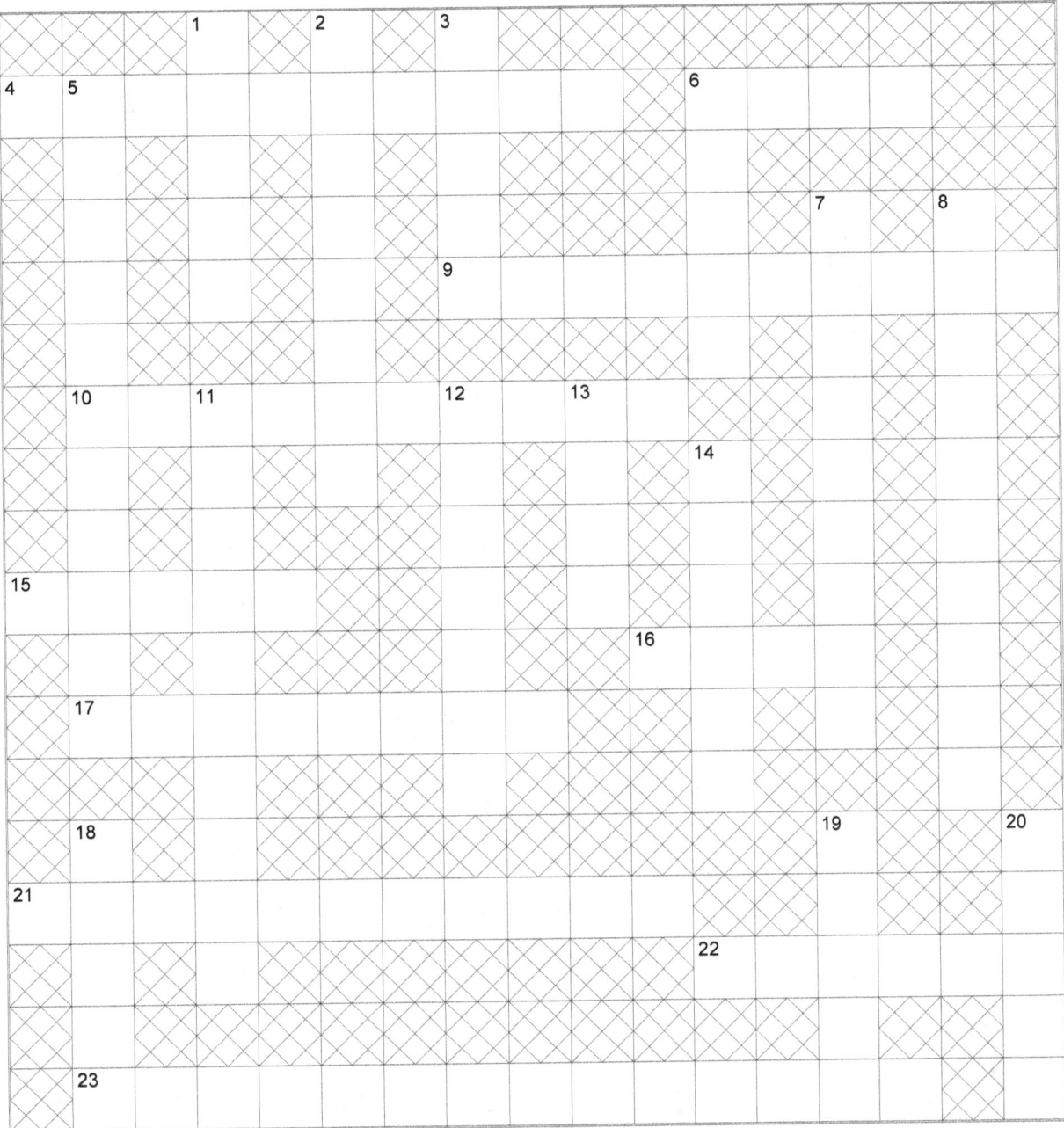

Across
4. Glasses
6. Neat
9. In a self-satisfied way
10. Image as from a mirror
15. Delay
16. Joy
17. Stems, shoots
21. Meddling, bothering, in the way
22. Weak
23. Full pants gathered below the knee

Down
1. Angry frown
2. Waterproof overshoes
3. Throw
5. Ghost that announces its presence
6. Short strands of hair
7. Snickered
8. Glittering
11. Intensely interested
12. Hesitantly
13. Sign
14. Grotesque elfin creature
18. Special talent
19. Scornful facial expression
20. Firm, severe

Sorcerer's Stone Vocabulary Crossword 3 Answer Key

			1 S		2 G		3 F				6			
4 S	5 P	E	C	T	A	C	L	E	S		T	I	D	Y
	O		O		L		I				U			
	L		W		O		N				F	7 S		8 G
	T		L		S	9 G	L	O	A	T	I	N	G	L	Y
	E				H						S	I		I
	10 R	E	11 F	L	E	C	12 T	I	13 O	N		G		S
	G		A		S		I		M	14 G		G		T
	E		S				M		E	O		E		E
15 H	I	T	C	H			I		N	B		R		N
	S		I				D		16 G	L	E	E		I
	17 T	E	N	D	R	I	L	S		I		D		N
			A				Y			N				G
	18 K		T									19 S		20 S
21 I	N	T	E	R	F	E	R	I	N	G		N		T
	A		D						22 F	E	E	B	L	E
	C											E		R
	23 K	N	I	C	K	E	R	B	O	C	K	E	R	S	N

Across
- 4. Glasses
- 6. Neat
- 9. In a self-satisfied way
- 10. Image as from a mirror
- 15. Delay
- 16. Joy
- 17. Stems, shoots
- 21. Meddling, bothering, in the way
- 22. Weak
- 23. Full pants gathered below the knee

Down
- 1. Angry frown
- 2. Waterproof overshoes
- 3. Throw
- 5. Ghost that announces its presence
- 6. Short strands of hair
- 7. Snickered
- 8. Glittering
- 11. Intensely interested
- 12. Hesitantly
- 13. Sign
- 14. Grotesque elfin creature
- 18. Special talent
- 19. Scornful facial expression
- 20. Firm, severe

Sorcerer's Stone Vocabulary Crossword 4

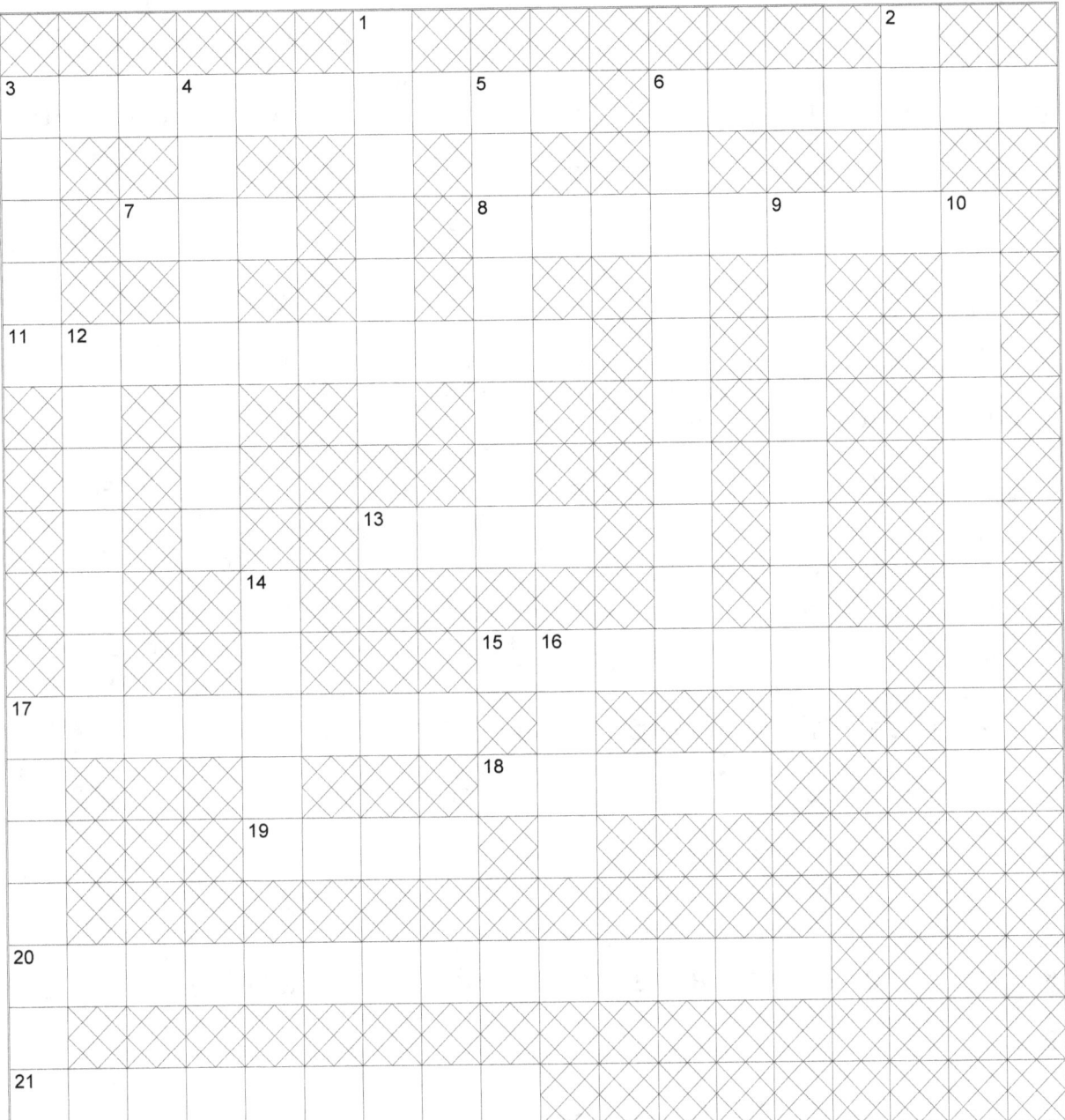

Across
- 3. Intensely interested
- 6. Growled
- 7. Tavern, bar
- 8. Paralyzed with terror
- 11. Reluctantly
- 13. Neat
- 15. Torn, mutilated
- 17. Cut, carved
- 18. Burdened
- 19. Witches
- 20. Full pants gathered below the knee
- 21. Nearly hopeless

Down
- 1. Moving gently
- 2. Joy
- 3. Throw
- 4. Large kettle for boiling
- 5. Forced, put out
- 6. Scraping
- 9. Not allowed
- 10. Dunce, dummy
- 12. Garbage, trash
- 14. Delay
- 16. Partially open
- 17. Struck, hit

Sorcerer's Stone Vocabulary Crossword 4 Answer Key

Across
- 3. Intensely interested
- 6. Growled
- 7. Tavern, bar
- 8. Paralyzed with terror
- 11. Reluctantly
- 13. Neat
- 15. Torn, mutilated
- 17. Cut, carved
- 18. Burdened
- 19. Witches
- 20. Full pants gathered below the knee
- 21. Nearly hopeless

Down
- 1. Moving gently
- 2. Joy
- 3. Throw
- 4. Large kettle for boiling
- 5. Forced, put out
- 6. Scraping
- 9. Not allowed
- 10. Dunce, dummy
- 12. Garbage, trash
- 14. Delay
- 16. Partially open
- 17. Struck, hit

Sorcerer's Stone Vocabulary Juggle Letters 1

1. RENSE = 1. _____
Scornful facial expression

2. EIRLNDEG = 2. _____
Delayed leaving

3. LEFEEB = 3. _____
Weak

4. RWZADI = 4. _____
Magician

5. DYTI = 5. _____
Neat

6. GAHHRNSTI = 6. _____
Beating, flailing

7. SOIFUYRUL = 7. _____
Angrily

8. LSHFFDUE = 8. _____
Walked while dragging feet

9. RFLGYUF = 9. _____
Harshly

10. MLOOGY = 10. _____
Dark, dreary

11. MENEMTAAZ = 11. _____
Wonder

12. PTEERUD = 12. _____
Burst, spewed

13. ULPPM = 13. _____
Chubby, full in figure

14. RSETN = 14. _____
Firm, severe

15. DRALCOUN = 15. _____
Large kettle for boiling

Sorcerer's Stone Vocabulary Juggle Letters 1 Answer Key

1. RENSE = 1. SNEER
Scornful facial expression

2. EIRLNDEG = 2. LINGERED
Delayed leaving

3. LEFEEB = 3. FEEBLE
Weak

4. RWZADI = 4. WIZARD
Magician

5. DYTI = 5. TIDY
Neat

6. GAHHRNSTI = 6. THRASHING
Beating, flailing

7. SOIFUYRUL = 7. FURIOUSLY
Angrily

8. LSHFFDUE = 8. SHUFFLED
Walked while dragging feet

9. RFLGYUF = 9. GRUFFLY
Harshly

10. MLOOGY = 10. GLOOMY
Dark, dreary

11. MENEMTAAZ = 11. AMAZEMENT
Wonder

12. PTEERUD = 12. ERUPTED
Burst, spewed

13. ULPPM = 13. PLUMP
Chubby, full in figure

14. RSETN = 14. STERN
Firm, severe

15. DRALCOUN = 15. CAULDRON
Large kettle for boiling

Sorcerer's Stone Vocabulary Juggle Letters 2

1. FYUFGRL = 1. _____
   Harshly

2. EGTESOTPILR = 2. _____
   Ghost that announces its presence

3. YRUF = 3. _____
   Intense anger, rage

4. TUSTF = 4. _____
   Short strands of hair

5. LUFDRFE = 5. _____
   Disturbed, annoyed

6. SKACLO = 6. _____
   Loose outer garments

7. ETREFPC = 7. _____
   Student officer

8. PUPLM = 8. _____
   Chubby, full in figure

9. ORIENCGW = 9. _____
   Cringing

10. MUROEONS = 10. _____
    Very big

11. CWLOS = 11. _____
    Angry frown

12. HSAG = 12. _____
    Witches

13. YLMGOO = 13. _____
    Dark, dreary

14. USBHRIB = 14. _____
    Garbage, trash

15. IOBNLG = 15. _____
    Grotesque elfin creature

Sorcerer's Stone Vocabulary Juggle Letters 2 Answer Key

1. FYUFGRL = 1. GRUFFLY
Harshly

2. EGTESOTPILR = 2. POLTERGEIST
Ghost that announces its presence

3. YRUF = 3. FURY
Intense anger, rage

4. TUSTF = 4. TUFTS
Short strands of hair

5. LUFDRFE = 5. RUFFLED
Disturbed, annoyed

6. SKACLO = 6. CLOAKS
Loose outer garments

7. ETREFPC = 7. PREFECT
Student officer

8. PUPLM = 8. PLUMP
Chubby, full in figure

9. ORIENCGW = 9. COWERING
Cringing

10. MUROEONS = 10. ENORMOUS
Very big

11. CWLOS = 11. SCOWL
Angry frown

12. HSAG = 12. HAGS
Witches

13. YLMGOO = 13. GLOOMY
Dark, dreary

14. USBHRIB = 14. RUBBISH
Garbage, trash

15. IOBNLG = 15. GOBLIN
Grotesque elfin creature

Sorcerer's Stone Vocabulary Juggle Letters 3

1. FOIEDRHRI = 1. _____
   Very shocked

2. LRFUFYG = 2. _____
   Harshly

3. MONE = 3. _____
   Sign

4. GNDREELI = 4. _____
   Delayed leaving

5. NARTMUT = 5. _____
   Fit

6. EDIUALQ = 6. _____
   Shrank in fear

7. NETZAEMAM = 7. _____
   Wonder

8. LNIBMUMG = 8. _____
   Speaking unclearly

9. LERDBEBOC = 9. _____
   Battered

10. AGHS = 10. _____
    Witches

11. EKEBCKIRRKNCOS = 11. _____
    Full pants gathered below the knee

12. KEDWCHA = 12. _____
    Struck, hit

13. GNLFI = 13. _____
    Throw

14. JRAA = 14. _____
    Partially open

15. RIEPFIDET = 15. _____
    Paralyzed with terror

Sorcerer's Stone Vocabulary Juggle Letters 3 Answer Key

1. FOIEDRHRI = 1. HORRIFIED
   Very shocked

2. LRFUFYG = 2. GRUFFLY
   Harshly

3. MONE = 3. OMEN
   Sign

4. GNDREELI = 4. LINGERED
   Delayed leaving

5. NARTMUT = 5. TANTRUM
   Fit

6. EDIUALQ = 6. QUAILED
   Shrank in fear

7. NETZAEMAM = 7. AMAZEMENT
   Wonder

8. LNIBMUMG = 8. MUMBLING
   Speaking unclearly

9. LERDBEBOC = 9. CLOBBERED
   Battered

10. AGHS =10. HAGS
    Witches

11. EKEBCKIRRKNCOS =11. KNICKERBOCKERS
    Full pants gathered below the knee

12. KEDWCHA =12. WHACKED
    Struck, hit

13. GNLFI =13. FLING
    Throw

14. JRAA =14. AJAR
    Partially open

15. RIEPFIDET =15. PETRIFIED
    Paralyzed with terror

Sorcerer's Stone Vocabulary Juggle Letters 4

1. UGNTRE = 1. _____
Needing immediate action

2. OKLSCA = 2. _____
Loose outer garments

3. EGNEGRIDS = 3. _____
Snickered

4. EEDREAPST = 4. _____
Nearly hopeless

5. LIGNOAGYLT = 5. _____
In a self-satisfied way

6. EESRN = 6. _____
Scornful facial expression

7. FRUELFD = 7. _____
Disturbed, annoyed

8. CENVDICON = 8. _____
Certain

9. CSDEKA = 9. _____
Fired, let go

10. LIGNF =10. _____
Throw

11. PINLGRAGP =11. _____
Struggling

12. SHOSEALG =12. _____
Waterproof overshoes

13. OIRDHFIRE =13. _____
Very shocked

14. IHWDETLT =14. _____
Cut, carved

15. IRNEDGLE =15. _____
Delayed leaving

Sorcerer's Stone Vocabulary Juggle Letters 4 Answer Key

1. UGNTRE = 1. URGENT
   Needing immediate action

2. OKLSCA = 2. CLOAKS
   Loose outer garments

3. EGNEGRIDS = 3. SNIGGERED
   Snickered

4. EEDREAPST = 4. DESPERATE
   Nearly hopeless

5. LIGNOAGYLT = 5. GLOATINGLY
   In a self-satisfied way

6. EESRN = 6. SNEER
   Scornful facial expression

7. FRUELFD = 7. RUFFLED
   Disturbed, annoyed

8. CENVDICON = 8. CONVINCED
   Certain

9. CSDEKA = 9. SACKED
   Fired, let go

10. LIGNF =10. FLING
    Throw

11. PINLGRAGP =11. GRAPPLING
    Struggling

12. SHOSEALG =12. GALOSHES
    Waterproof overshoes

13. OIRDHFIRE =13. HORRIFIED
    Very shocked

14. IHWDETLT =14. WHITTLED
    Cut, carved

15. IRNEDGLE =15. LINGERED
    Delayed leaving

Copyrighted

AGONY	Extreme pain
AJAR	Partially open
AMAZEMENT	Wonder
BABBLE	Foolish talk
BIASED	Prejudiced
BLURTED	Said impulsively

BURLY	Husky
CAULDRON	Large kettle for boiling
CLAMBERED	Climbed with difficulty
CLOAKS	Loose outer garments
CLOBBERED	Battered
CONVINCED	Certain

COWERING	Cringing
CRANING	Stretching, straining
CRINKLED	Wrinkled
DANGLING	Hanging loosely
DESPERATE	Nearly hopeless
DESTINY	Fate

DUNDERHEAD	Dunce, dummy
ELIXIR	Special medicine
ENORMOUS	Very big
ERUPTED	Burst, spewed
EXPELLED	Forced, put out
FASCINATED	Intensely interested

FEEBLE	Weak
FLINCHED	Winced
FLING	Throw
FORBIDDEN	Not allowed
FURIOUSLY	Angrily
FURY	Intense anger, rage

GALOSHES	Waterproof overshoes
GLEE	Joy
GLISTENING	Glittering
GLOATINGLY	In a self-satisfied way
GLOOMY	Dark, dreary
GOBLIN	Grotesque elfin creature

GOGGLE	Stare
GRAPPLING	Struggling
GRUDGINGLY	Reluctantly
GRUFFLY	Harshly
HAGS	Witches
HITCH	Delay

HORRIFIED	Very shocked
HOVERING	Floating suspended in air
INSTINCT	Natural behavior
INTERFERING	Meddling, bothering, in the way
JOSTLED	Pushed, elbowed
KNACK	Special talent

KNICKERBOCKERS	Full pants gathered below the knee
LADEN	Burdened
LINGERED	Delayed leaving
MANGLED	Torn, mutilated
MIFFED	Annoyed
MUMBLING	Speaking unclearly

MUTELY	Silently
MYSTIFIED	Bewildered, perplexed
OMEN	Sign
PECULIAR	Odd, unusual
PELTING	Hurling
PETRIFIED	Paralyzed with terror

PLUMP	Chubby, full in figure
POLTERGEIST	Ghost that announces its presence
PREFECT	Student officer
PUB	Tavern, bar
QUAILED	Shrank in fear
REFLECTION	Image as from a mirror

REMORSE	Regret
RUBBISH	Garbage, trash
RUFFLED	Disturbed, annoyed
SACKED	Fired, let go
SAVAGING	Attacking violently
SCOWL	Angry frown

SCRABBLING	Scraping
SEIZED	Grabbed
SHUDDERED	Shivered, as from fear or aversion
SHUFFLED	Walked while dragging feet
SLITHER	Slide, glide
SNARLED	Growled

SNEER	Scornful facial expression
SNIGGERED	Snickered
SPECTACLES	Glasses
STERN	Firm, severe
SUPPOSED	Assumed to be true
TANTRUM	Fit

TENDRILS	Stems, shoots
TIDY	Neat
TIMIDLY	Hesitantly
THRASHING	Beating, flailing
TRODDEN	Walked on
TUFTS	Short strands of hair

URGENT	Needing immediate action
WAFTING	Moving gently
WHACKED	Struck, hit
WHEELED	Turned suddenly
WHITTLED	Cut, carved
WIZARD	Magician

Sorcerer's Stone Vocabulary

KNICKERBOCKERS	RUBBISH	BLURTED	CLOAKS	CLAMBERED
WHACKED	SLITHER	WHITTLED	INTERFERING	FASCINATED
SUPPOSED	POLTERGEIST	FREE SPACE	SNIGGERED	REFLECTION
AJAR	TIDY	MUMBLING	SCRABBLING	BABBLE
SACKED	MYSTIFIED	GOGGLE	SEIZED	OMEN

Sorcerer's Stone Vocabulary

MUTELY	FLINCHED	SHUDDERED	SPECTACLES	GOBLIN
GLOOMY	PUB	PELTING	HAGS	JOSTLED
PREFECT	FURIOUSLY	FREE SPACE	TENDRILS	LADEN
CRINKLED	GRAPPLING	BIASED	CLOBBERED	WHEELED
KNACK	THRASHING	HOVERING	GALOSHES	PETRIFIED

Sorcerer's Stone Vocabulary

PUB	GRAPPLING	SACKED	ERUPTED	TANTRUM
LINGERED	INSTINCT	RUBBISH	EXPELLED	MUMBLING
DESPERATE	HORRIFIED	FREE SPACE	REFLECTION	TRODDEN
PETRIFIED	SLITHER	GRUDGINGLY	ELIXIR	GLOOMY
URGENT	MUTELY	WHEELED	QUAILED	ENORMOUS

Sorcerer's Stone Vocabulary

BABBLE	HOVERING	CRANING	TUFTS	POLTERGEIST
REMORSE	FURIOUSLY	GRUFFLY	OMEN	CRINKLED
GLEE	CLAMBERED	FREE SPACE	MYSTIFIED	CONVINCED
PREFECT	AJAR	DANGLING	SNARLED	AGONY
WIZARD	BURLY	FLING	STERN	CLOBBERED

Sorcerer's Stone Vocabulary

CLOAKS	HOVERING	ELIXIR	PREFECT	TRODDEN
MUTELY	SLITHER	TANTRUM	INTERFERING	HORRIFIED
GRUFFLY	AMAZEMENT	FREE SPACE	FLINCHED	PECULIAR
WIZARD	URGENT	SEIZED	BIASED	GRAPPLING
WHITTLED	EXPELLED	GLOATINGLY	SCRABBLING	GOGGLE

Sorcerer's Stone Vocabulary

SAVAGING	SPECTACLES	DANGLING	REMORSE	CAULDRON
RUBBISH	MIFFED	PLUMP	WHACKED	CLOBBERED
GLISTENING	SACKED	FREE SPACE	MANGLED	MYSTIFIED
HAGS	GLOOMY	GOBLIN	PELTING	THRASHING
FURIOUSLY	GLEE	TIDY	COWERING	TENDRILS

Sorcerer's Stone Vocabulary

FURY	EXPELLED	BIASED	FORBIDDEN	FEEBLE
ELIXIR	GLOATINGLY	CLOAKS	SAVAGING	CLAMBERED
INSTINCT	SEIZED	FREE SPACE	CLOBBERED	RUFFLED
MUTELY	DESTINY	PUB	BLURTED	SNARLED
BURLY	SNIGGERED	SHUFFLED	BABBLE	CONVINCED

Sorcerer's Stone Vocabulary

REFLECTION	HORRIFIED	SCOWL	SNEER	GLEE
TIMIDLY	MANGLED	SPECTACLES	GRUFFLY	CRINKLED
WAFTING	ERUPTED	FREE SPACE	GOBLIN	WHACKED
PELTING	HAGS	HITCH	REMORSE	CRANING
WIZARD	HOVERING	DUNDERHEAD	GRUDGINGLY	LADEN

Sorcerer's Stone Vocabulary

QUAILED	HAGS	REFLECTION	CONVINCED	GLISTENING
PETRIFIED	DANGLING	DESTINY	MUTELY	LINGERED
GLEE	SHUDDERED	FREE SPACE	PREFECT	CLOAKS
GOGGLE	BIASED	JOSTLED	GLOOMY	GLOATINGLY
ENORMOUS	PELTING	RUBBISH	DUNDERHEAD	DESPERATE

Sorcerer's Stone Vocabulary

TUFTS	AMAZEMENT	FURIOUSLY	CLAMBERED	CLOBBERED
SHUFFLED	SNIGGERED	CRINKLED	KNICKERBOCKERS	WHEELED
SCRABBLING	KNACK	FREE SPACE	WHACKED	EXPELLED
CAULDRON	WAFTING	BABBLE	BURLY	FLING
MYSTIFIED	SAVAGING	TENDRILS	SCOWL	CRANING

Sorcerer's Stone Vocabulary

MUMBLING	MUTELY	SACKED	ENORMOUS	FURIOUSLY
TRODDEN	CLOBBERED	TANTRUM	ELIXIR	SHUDDERED
BABBLE	SNEER	FREE SPACE	DANGLING	SUPPOSED
GLOATINGLY	FASCINATED	LADEN	PELTING	URGENT
SHUFFLED	INSTINCT	BLURTED	THRASHING	WAFTING

Sorcerer's Stone Vocabulary

CAULDRON	KNICKERBOCKERS	FLINCHED	CRANING	RUBBISH
INTERFERING	WHACKED	MIFFED	KNACK	PECULIAR
EXPELLED	GLOOMY	FREE SPACE	HOVERING	AJAR
SPECTACLES	CRINKLED	GRAPPLING	DESPERATE	SLITHER
PETRIFIED	SCRABBLING	WHITTLED	FLING	GALOSHES

Sorcerer's Stone Vocabulary

COWERING	GRUFFLY	OMEN	CAULDRON	DESPERATE
SAVAGING	HOVERING	CRANING	ENORMOUS	SPECTACLES
SNIGGERED	URGENT	FREE SPACE	DANGLING	PECULIAR
GRUDGINGLY	WHITTLED	GLOATINGLY	INTERFERING	WIZARD
FASCINATED	GLEE	AMAZEMENT	PETRIFIED	TIMIDLY

Sorcerer's Stone Vocabulary

BURLY	AGONY	SCRABBLING	CONVINCED	INSTINCT
LADEN	ERUPTED	TENDRILS	KNICKERBOCKERS	GALOSHES
SLITHER	DUNDERHEAD	FREE SPACE	FLING	SNARLED
FORBIDDEN	STERN	MIFFED	MUMBLING	MYSTIFIED
SUPPOSED	FURIOUSLY	LINGERED	SCOWL	PLUMP

Sorcerer's Stone Vocabulary

TUFTS	ELIXIR	PLUMP	QUAILED	AGONY
RUBBISH	CRANING	TIDY	TRODDEN	GOBLIN
SACKED	ERUPTED	FREE SPACE	PREFECT	GRAPPLING
GOGGLE	SAVAGING	FLING	AMAZEMENT	MIFFED
WHITTLED	WHEELED	PETRIFIED	THRASHING	SHUDDERED

Sorcerer's Stone Vocabulary

SPECTACLES	SUPPOSED	CAULDRON	LINGERED	TANTRUM
CLAMBERED	SCRABBLING	BURLY	GLISTENING	OMEN
SLITHER	SHUFFLED	FREE SPACE	CLOBBERED	SNEER
CLOAKS	KNICKERBOCKERS	ENORMOUS	DANGLING	COWERING
GRUDGINGLY	POLTERGEIST	DESPERATE	SNARLED	URGENT

Sorcerer's Stone Vocabulary

FURIOUSLY	AJAR	GOGGLE	WHEELED	MUMBLING
JOSTLED	SHUFFLED	SAVAGING	QUAILED	RUBBISH
CLOBBERED	PELTING	FREE SPACE	INSTINCT	REFLECTION
TRODDEN	PECULIAR	FEEBLE	HITCH	URGENT
GALOSHES	WAFTING	TUFTS	CRINKLED	FORBIDDEN

Sorcerer's Stone Vocabulary

RUFFLED	PETRIFIED	PUB	SUPPOSED	CLOAKS
GRUFFLY	SLITHER	KNACK	BLURTED	SCOWL
LADEN	HAGS	FREE SPACE	TENDRILS	CRANING
CLAMBERED	TANTRUM	PREFECT	MIFFED	SNEER
AMAZEMENT	CONVINCED	GRAPPLING	GLOATINGLY	AGONY

Sorcerer's Stone Vocabulary

GLOOMY	FASCINATED	GRUDGINGLY	WAFTING	MUMBLING
WHACKED	POLTERGEIST	BABBLE	FURY	INSTINCT
HOVERING	MIFFED	FREE SPACE	LINGERED	GLEE
TUFTS	REMORSE	BIASED	RUFFLED	CRINKLED
STERN	DUNDERHEAD	CLAMBERED	TIMIDLY	THRASHING

Sorcerer's Stone Vocabulary

SHUFFLED	SCOWL	FLINCHED	PUB	GLISTENING
INTERFERING	SNEER	ELIXIR	DANGLING	AGONY
ERUPTED	COWERING	FREE SPACE	FLING	REFLECTION
DESTINY	OMEN	GOBLIN	BLURTED	GLOATINGLY
PETRIFIED	WIZARD	KNICKERBOCKERS	CLOAKS	CRANING

Sorcerer's Stone Vocabulary

WAFTING	WHACKED	DUNDERHEAD	BABBLE	SCRABBLING
WIZARD	ENORMOUS	CRANING	HITCH	PREFECT
SPECTACLES	DESTINY	FREE SPACE	ERUPTED	BIASED
FURY	MYSTIFIED	HORRIFIED	AMAZEMENT	WHITTLED
TRODDEN	GRAPPLING	CAULDRON	CLOBBERED	CONVINCED

Sorcerer's Stone Vocabulary

GLISTENING	FORBIDDEN	MUTELY	MANGLED	DESPERATE
STERN	CLAMBERED	TANTRUM	TIMIDLY	FEEBLE
GLOOMY	THRASHING	FREE SPACE	FLING	TENDRILS
ELIXIR	SLITHER	PECULIAR	POLTERGEIST	INTERFERING
LADEN	SEIZED	FLINCHED	SNIGGERED	PUB

Sorcerer's Stone Vocabulary

SCRABBLING	URGENT	BLURTED	TIMIDLY	SUPPOSED
MUTELY	WAFTING	FURY	INTERFERING	FASCINATED
CONVINCED	PREFECT	FREE SPACE	ELIXIR	BURLY
WHITTLED	SLITHER	FORBIDDEN	GRUFFLY	SAVAGING
EXPELLED	PLUMP	RUFFLED	SEIZED	FURIOUSLY

Sorcerer's Stone Vocabulary

QUAILED	MYSTIFIED	AJAR	DANGLING	AGONY
SACKED	FLINCHED	WHACKED	OMEN	DESTINY
GLEE	HAGS	FREE SPACE	TANTRUM	CLAMBERED
HOVERING	LINGERED	GOGGLE	COWERING	SNEER
MANGLED	GRUDGINGLY	CLOAKS	WHEELED	BIASED

Sorcerer's Stone Vocabulary

RUBBISH	INSTINCT	INTERFERING	LINGERED	TANTRUM
SHUFFLED	ENORMOUS	COWERING	BIASED	ELIXIR
FURY	SHUDDERED	FREE SPACE	GOBLIN	FEEBLE
SCOWL	TIDY	WIZARD	THRASHING	REMORSE
QUAILED	ERUPTED	KNICKERBOCKERS	SNEER	SNARLED

Sorcerer's Stone Vocabulary

HAGS	DESPERATE	MYSTIFIED	KNACK	JOSTLED
MANGLED	TUFTS	PLUMP	GLEE	MIFFED
DUNDERHEAD	TENDRILS	FREE SPACE	URGENT	WHEELED
GRAPPLING	GRUFFLY	AGONY	SLITHER	GOGGLE
SPECTACLES	AJAR	GALOSHES	PELTING	FORBIDDEN

Sorcerer's Stone Vocabulary

FLING	STERN	GRUDGINGLY	FURY	GOGGLE
REFLECTION	PUB	TENDRILS	SEIZED	CRANING
ELIXIR	DESPERATE	FREE SPACE	BABBLE	CRINKLED
SAVAGING	OMEN	SCOWL	MYSTIFIED	AGONY
PELTING	FLINCHED	GRUFFLY	BIASED	PECULIAR

Sorcerer's Stone Vocabulary

TIMIDLY	TUFTS	BLURTED	RUFFLED	CAULDRON
HAGS	REMORSE	FASCINATED	ERUPTED	GLEE
JOSTLED	URGENT	FREE SPACE	SNIGGERED	GRAPPLING
TANTRUM	CLOAKS	SPECTACLES	LINGERED	GLOOMY
GALOSHES	AMAZEMENT	DUNDERHEAD	SLITHER	SACKED

Sorcerer's Stone Vocabulary

SAVAGING	MUTELY	WIZARD	AJAR	SNARLED
JOSTLED	ELIXIR	MIFFED	HITCH	PLUMP
PECULIAR	GALOSHES	FREE SPACE	TIDY	DESPERATE
THRASHING	GOGGLE	SCRABBLING	WHEELED	REFLECTION
SNEER	PELTING	LINGERED	DESTINY	DANGLING

Sorcerer's Stone Vocabulary

FURIOUSLY	CAULDRON	SEIZED	GRUDGINGLY	HAGS
TIMIDLY	GLOATINGLY	AMAZEMENT	GRAPPLING	SPECTACLES
QUAILED	INTERFERING	FREE SPACE	SHUFFLED	CLOBBERED
TENDRILS	CRINKLED	BIASED	TRODDEN	KNACK
FORBIDDEN	LADEN	HOVERING	FASCINATED	GLEE

Sorcerer's Stone Vocabulary

MUTELY	MIFFED	DESPERATE	LINGERED	CLOAKS
TENDRILS	PECULIAR	WHACKED	FORBIDDEN	SLITHER
GLOOMY	SAVAGING	FREE SPACE	TIMIDLY	BABBLE
WIZARD	ERUPTED	TIDY	FASCINATED	SPECTACLES
SCOWL	EXPELLED	ELIXIR	CLOBBERED	GOGGLE

Sorcerer's Stone Vocabulary

COWERING	KNICKERBOCKERS	STERN	INSTINCT	PETRIFIED
GRUDGINGLY	RUBBISH	HITCH	HOVERING	REMORSE
FLINCHED	BURLY	FREE SPACE	QUAILED	PREFECT
PELTING	LADEN	SHUDDERED	URGENT	TUFTS
KNACK	RUFFLED	POLTERGEIST	AGONY	SHUFFLED

www.ingramcontent.com/pod-product-compliance
Lightning Source LLC
Chambersburg PA
CBHW081452070526
44586CB00019B/2314